Essays on the Ancient Semitic World

EDITED BY
J. W. WEVERS AND
D. B. REDFORD

UNIVERSITY OF TORONTO PRESS

Printed in Belgium for
University of Toronto Press
Toronto and Buffalo

ISBN 0-8020-1603-0

ESSAYS ON THE ANCIENT SEMITIC WORLD

TORONTO SEMITIC TEXTS AND STUDIES

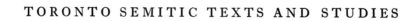

Preface

During these middle decades of the twentieth century, when each scholary discipline has long since turned in upon itself and become highly specialized, the search is for some means of liaison among virtually isolated groups. More and more the need has been felt by the individual scholar to pool his resources with those of his colleagues. Otherwise, so runs the tacitly accepted reasoning, we must all wedge ourselves tighter and tighter into narrow passages where no forward movement is possible. The great advantage in a college of scholars in which free exchange of ideas is not only possible, but shrewdly encouraged, is that such impasses are never reached. Of course, no matter how freely departments are allowed to intermingle the unknown psychological factor may effectively nullify any fruitful fellowship above the purely social level. In this case kindness and understanding are the only weapons of combat. Nevertheless a scholar's intellect tells him that he should exchange ideas with his fellows; for the field of scholarly endeavour is not segmented into watertight compartments, but resembles the broad expanse of the rainbow, where colours melt into one another, and sharp lines are never certain. In an atmosphere like this, unless he is to attempt the impossible role of an erudite Pooh-bah, a scholar is obliged to enter into constant communication with his colleagues who command a knowledge of those disciplines which touch upon and overlap his own. The traditional picture of the lone scholar, doing his work by himself in his garret, must be replaced by the image of the dialogue or seminar. Both dialogue and seminar must inevitably cut across traditional lines to recruit participants from seemingly far-flung fields. For example, it is difficult to imagine how today a student of the Egyptian language could proceed at all without the help of a linguist; or how a student of Egyptian religion could accomplish anything which is not superficial unless he be assisted by one versed in the history of religions, or possess such training himself. Can the Hittitologist do without the help of his brother, the Assyriologist? Can the student of the Aegean Bronze Age dispense with a detailed knowledge of Levantine history and archaeology?

Departments are needed which bring together men of diverse training, and though such department labels as "Mediterranean Studies" or "Ancient History" might sound bizarre to scholars of a bygone age, they are very much a sign of the times of today.

The Department of Near Eastern Studies at the University of Toronto constitutes just such an aggregation of diverse specialists. The volume of papers published herewith fulfils at least partly a hope which the editors have long entertained, viz. of setting forth in a publication peculiarly its own something of the researches being carried on by these scholars. The seven contributors to the present work are all either graduates, or members, of the department, and their writings represent a cross-section of the wide range of disciplines they command as a group. Although, like most similar departments in other universities, the Toronto Department of Near Eastern Studies began its life in the preceding century devoted wholly to Hebraic studies, the door has long since been opened to other interests. Today studies in Assyriology, Egyptology, Septuagint and Hellenistic Greek, Aramaic, Syriac, linguistics and pre-Islamic Arabia are all firmly ensconced beside the study of the Old Testament. Moreover, thanks to the warm co-operation between the Department and the Royal Ontario Museum, it is now possible to add Near Eastern archaeology to this growing list. The Department has contributed personnel to several Near Eastern "digs," including the excavations of the British School of Archaeology at Jericho and Jerusalem, and J. B. Pritchard's excavation at Gibeon; and two of its members have held the post of director of the American Schools of Oriental Research in Jerusalem.

It has been decided to confine the present volume to Semitica and related fields of non-biblical interest. By adopting the title "Texts and Studies" the editors intended to call forth papers of two kinds: (*a*) publications of inscriptions, reliefs, manuscripts, tablets, papyri, and graffiti, and (*b*) definitive studies of problems arising out of similar texts already published.

Two papers deal with Akkadian materials, five with Hebrew, and one with Egyptian. Professors Grayson and Sweet respectively offer new information on Assyrian hunters and the publication of an interesting Neo-Babylonian incantation text in the Royal Ontario Museum. Professor Culley suggests a new approach to the measurement of metre in classical Hebrew poetry, and Professor Williams writes on the passive of the *Qal* in Hebrew. Two papers belong to the realm of Hebrew phonetics. Professor Revell's detailed paper on the vocalization of Hebrew is a definitive study of the first rank, and

Professor Wevers' treatment of the Greek transcription of the Hebrew letter *ḥeth* in the LXX is an important contribution to the phonology of Hebrew in the second century B.C. The lone Egyptian contribution by Professor Redford deals with an inscribed relief of a fan-bearer in the Royal Ontario Museum.

This work has been published with the help of a grant from the Humanities Research Council of Canada using funds provided by the Canada Council.

JUNE 1966

J.W.W.
D.B.R.

Contents

Sigla

ABL	R. F. Harper, *Assyrian and Babylonian Letters*, I–XIV (London and Chicago, 1892–1914)
AHw	W. von Soden, *Akkadisches Handwörterbuch* (Wiesbaden, 1959)
AJSL	*American Journal of Semitic Languages and Literature*
AKA	E. A. W. Budge and L. W. King, *The Annals of the Kings of Assyria* (London, 1902)
AOS	*The American Oriental Series*
ASAE	*Annales du Service des antiquités de l'Égypte*
Arch. f. Or.	*Archiv für Orientforschung*
BA	*Beiträge zur Assyriologie*
BBR	H. Zimmern, *Beiträge zur Kenntnis der babylonischen Religion*, I (Leipzig, 1896), II (Leipzig, 1901)
BIFAO	*Bulletin de l'Institut français d'archéologie orientale*
BWANT	*Beiträge zur Wissenschaft vom alten und neuen Testament*
CAD	*Chicago Assyrian Dictionary* (Chicago and Glückstadt, 1956)
CdE	*Chronique d'Égypte*
CH	*Code of Hammurabi*
EA	El-Amarna
FF Communications	*Folklore Fellows, Communications*, Academica Scientiarum Sennica, Helsinki
Gilg.	*Gilgamesh Epic*
HUCA	*Hebrew Union College Annual*
JBL	*Journal of Biblical Literature*
JEA	*Journal of Egyptian Archaeology*
JNES	*Journal of Near Eastern Studies*
JQR	*Jewish Quarterly Review*
JSS	*Journal of Semitic Studies*
KAH	*Keilschrifttexte aus Assur historischen Inhalts*
KAI	H. Donner and W. Röllig, *Kanaanäische und aramäische Inschriften* (3 vols.; Wiesbaden, 1962–4)
LSS	*Leipziger semitische Studien*
LTBA	*Die lexikalischen Tafelserien der Babylonier und Assyrer*, I, II (Berlin, 1933)
MAOG	*Mitteilungen der altorientalischen Gesellschaft*

MIFAO	*Mémoires de l'Institut français d'archéologie orientale*
MT	Masoretic Text
Or.	*Orientalia*
RdE	*Revue d'Égyptologie*
REA	*Revue de l'Égypte ancienne*
Sam. Pent.	Samaritan Pentateuch
STC	L. W. King, *The Seven Tablets of Creation*, I, II (London, 1902)
STT	O. R. Gurney and J. J. Finkelstein, *The Sultantepe Tablets*, I (London, 1957)
VAB	*Vorderasiatische Bibliothek*
VT	*Vetus Testamentum*
WO	*Die Welt des Orients*
WZKM	*Wiener Zeitschrift für die Kunde des Morgenlandes*
ZA	*Zeitschrift für Assyriologie*
ZAW	*Zeitschrift für die alttestamentliche Wissenschaft*
ZÄS	*Zeitschrift für ägyptische Sprache und Altertumskunde*
ZDMG	*Zeitschrift der deutschen morgenländischen Gesellschaft*

ESSAYS ON THE ANCIENT SEMITIC WORLD

New Evidence on an Assyrian Hunting Practice

A. K. GRAYSON

In a previous article the author proposed that an enigmatic word in the Assyrian royal annals which had to do with hunting should be read *šubtu* and suggested as its meaning "animal pit."[1] It now appears that the *šubtu* is actually depicted in an Assyrian relief from Aššurbanipal's palace. The sculpture is badly broken and only drawings of the relevant two pieces[2] had previously been published.[3] A photograph of the fragments is published here for the first time with the permission of the Trustees of the British Museum. Since the sculpture is to be included in a collection of Aššurbanipal reliefs being prepared by Dr. R. D. Barnett, the author will confine himself here to a brief discussion of the significance of the scene as a possible representation of the *šubtu*.

The relief shows a hunter, presumably Aššurbanipal, together with a squire crouched in a deep pit. The hunter has drawn his bow to release an arrow at gazelles. The animals have obviously been taken by surprise. One is still running towards the pit while a

1 A. K. Grayson, "Ambush and Animal Pit in Akkadian," *Studies Presented to A. Leo Oppenheim* (Chicago, 1964), pp. 90–4. The first two sentences in the last paragraph on p. 92 should read: "The phrase *ana kakki kamāsu* ('to bow down to the weapon' or perhaps 'to rally to the weapon' – von Soden, *AHw*, p. 431) is otherwise unknown. The sign DIŠ is inexplicable." For a correction to the translation of *ABL* 138 (quoted on p. 90) as well as the additional passage *ABL* 1263: 5–13 (and possibly *ABL* 705 r. 12), see K. H. Deller, *Or.* n.s. 34 (1965), p. 74, n. 3.

2 BM 124872 and 124873.

3 A drawing of BM 124872 was published by C. J. Gadd, *The Stones of Assyria* (London, 1936), pl. 30. Both pieces were earlier published by V. Place, *Ninive et l'Assyrie* (see Gadd, *op. cit.*, p. 184 for the exact reference). This latter work was not at the disposal of the present author.

second has turned and is fleeing in the opposite direction with an arrow lodged in its left shoulder. It is about to be struck by a second arrow. The fact that the hunter is in a pit and that the gazelles have been taken by surprise indicates this has been an ambush. One may assume that while the hunter and his servant have lain hidden in the pit, the gazelles have been driven in this direction by battue.[4] As soon as they were within range the hunter raised himself and began to shoot his arrows as quickly as possible.

The arrangement is reminiscent of the statements concerning the hunting device called *šubtu* in the Assyrian royal annals. It is therefore proposed, in accordance with a suggestion of Dr. Barnett, that this relief does in fact portray the *šubtu*. In the author's original proposal it was assumed that the *šubtu* was intended for the animals and thus it was translated "animal pit." From the relief, however, it appears that the *šubtu* was intended for the hunter and so the translation should be "ambush pit."[5] Yet another possibility is that *šubtu* refers to the practice as a whole rather than specifically to the pit. If this is the case, it should be translated "ambush" as it is in military contexts.

The translations of the passages in the Assyrian royal annals in which *šubtu* occurs should therefore be changed:

30 *pirāni*^{meš} *ina šub-ti a-duk*
I killed thirty elephants from an ambush pit.[6]

29 *pirāni*^{meš} *ina šub-ti a-di*
I drove[7] twenty-nine elephants into an ambush.[8]

6 *pirāni*^{meš} *ina me-it-ḫu-ṣi a-duk* x [*ina*] ^{SAL}*šub-te lu ad-di* 4 *pirāni*^{meš} *balṭūti*^{meš} *aṣ-bat* 5 *ina kip-pi aṣ-bat*
I killed six elephants in a conflict, I drove . . . [into] an ambush, I captured four elephants alive, I captured five by means of a snare.[9]

4 Gadd, *op. cit.*, p. 184. Battue is also indicated by the verb *nadû* which is used with *šubtu* in the Assyrian annals. See below.

5 Note the lexical passage where the singular *šūšubtum*, which denotes some kind of seat, is equated to *kussû šapiltum* (Grayson, "Ambush," p. 93). To the lexical passages quoted on p. 93 add: *š*[*u*]*-šub-tú* = *nar-kab-tú*, W. von Soden, *LTBA* 2, 1 vi 34 = 2:371, and cf. B. Meissner, *MAOG* 11 (1937), p. 77, who thinks it refers to a wagon seat. The author wishes to thank D. J. Wiseman for this reference.

6 *AKA*, p. 205 iv 70–2 (Aššur-nāṣir-apli II).

7 For *nadû*, "to drive (animals)," also note *CH* § 58.

8 *Sumer* 6 (1950), p. 18 iv 44 (= *WO* 1 [1947–52], p. 472), also *KAH* 2, no. 112 r. 11 (= *WO* 1 [1947–52], p. 9) (Šalmaneser III). The author is indebted to D. J. Wiseman for the reference to *Sumer* 6. In *WO* 1 (1947–52), p. 472, the numeral is to be corrected. It is 29, not 23, as is clear from the photograph in *Sumer* 6 (1950), pl. II. (Three vertical wedges placed on top of one another represent 9, not 3.)

9 *KAH* 2, no. 84 r. 125 (= J. Seidmann, *MAOG* 9/3 [1935], pp. 34f.) (Adad-

124873

The passage from the annals of Aššur-dān II is to be omitted since *šubtu* is not actually preserved in the original.[10] Note that the three occurrences of *šubtu* in the Assyrian royal annals all have to do with elephant-hunting. This fact may be attributed to the chance of discovery and cannot be regarded as a serious objection to the identification of the Aššurbanipal relief, which has to do with the hunting of gazelles. There is apparently no published text of Aššurbanipal which refers to this scene or even to the hunting of gazelles. Only lion-hunting plays a major role in this king's inscriptions.[11]

Even though one must apparently abandon the idea that the *šubtu* is an animal pit, it should be noted that words for animal pit are still attested in Akkadian. In the Gilgameš Epic two words with this meaning are used, *būru* and *šuttu*.[12]

In conclusion it appears that the word *šubtu* in hunting contexts refers to the practice of the hunter shooting from a hidden depression[13] in the ground at animals which have been driven towards him. Whether *šubtu* refers specifically to the pit (and therefore is to be translated "ambush pit") or to the whole arrangement (and therefore is to be translated simply as "ambush" as it is in military contexts) is uncertain. In either case the scene portrayed in the fragmentary relief published here is almost certainly to be connected with the word *šubtu*.[14]

---

nērāri II). In the author's original article note the typographical error in the transliteration: [SA]*šub-te* for [SAL]*šub-te*.

10 In his transliteration E. Weidner (*Arch. f. Or.* 3 [1926], p. 160 r. 26f.) reads: [. . . i-n](a *šub*-te) ú-ṣab-bi-ta. The fact that *šubte* is restored, along with what precedes *ina*, is not clear from his footnote (n. 7), but is clear when one looks at the copy on p. 155. The present author doubts, in fact, that Weidner's *ina šubte* is the correct restoration here since otherwise *šubtu* is not attested with the verb *ṣubbutu* (only with *dâku* and *nadû*).

11 M. Streck, *VAB* 7/2, pp. 304–11.

12 The passages in which *būru* occurs were quoted in the original article on p. 94. For *šuttu* note:

tarâmīma nēša gāmir (variant: *migir*) *emūqē*
tuḫtarrīššu 7 *u* 7 *šuttāti*

You (Ištar) used to love the omnipotent lion,
Then you had dug for him seven and (again) seven pits.

Gilg. VI 51–52, variant from P. Garelli, *Gilgameš et sa légende* (Paris, 1960), p. 120 ii 17f.

13 There is no evidence to indicate whether the pit was a natural depression in the ground or whether it was man-made.

14 W. G. Lambert, after reading this article in manuscript, suggested that, from a practical point of view, the hunting of elephants from a pit would involve serious risks for the hunter. Some of the elephants from a stampeding herd might tumble into the pit and crush the occupant. In view of this consideration the word *šubtu*, at least when used with reference to elephant-hunting (as in military contexts), may simply refer to ambush in general rather than to a specific method of ambush.

An Akkadian Incantation Text

R. F. G. SWEET

Cuneiform tablet D. 988 in the Royal Ontario Museum, Toronto, here published by permission of T. Cuyler Young, Jr., Associate Curator in charge of the West Asian Department of the museum, was acquired by purchase in May 1925. Nothing can be said about its ultimate provenance, other than what one may care to infer from the fact that the script is Neo-Babylonian. It contains two incantation prayers, one, running to thirteen lines, addressed to "the god of the house and the goddess of the house," and the other, running to sixteen lines, addressed to Šamaš; each prayer is introduced by four lines of ritual directions, and two lines of similar content form the conclusion. The purpose of the rituals and prayers was to enable a man to ward off some evil which an ill omen had shown to be threatening him.

Despite several valuable suggestions for the understanding of the text received from Erica Reiner and Wilfred G. Lambert, to whom grateful acknowledgment is here expressed, completely satisfactory sense has not been made of every line, particularly the incomplete lines of the first prayer, and it has not been possible to restore every lacuna.

TRANSLITERATION

Obverse

1 [x x x x x x x x x] ⌜x x x⌝ *ma* ⌜x x x⌝ [x]
2 [x x x x x x] ⌜x x x x x x x x⌝ [x x x]
3 ⌜x⌝ [x x x] ⌜^{d}INNIN⌝ É ⌜x x x⌝ *ú* [x x x x]
4 *ina* ⌜KÁ⌝ É-*šú* ⌜NÍG⌝.NA ⌜ŠIM⌝.LI GAR-*an* UR$_5$.⌜GIM⌝ DUG$_4$.[GA]

---

5 ⌜DINGIR⌝ É ^{d}INNIN É ⌜x⌝ [x x x x x x]
6 ⌜*mu-deš*⌝-[*š*]*u-ú zi*-⌜*e*⌝-*ri* [x x x x x x x]
7 ⌜*taḫ*⌝-*da-a-ma ni-iḫ-ta-di ki* [x x x x x]
8 ⌜*ta-aš*⌝-*ru-ka* GISKIM *la ḫa-di-e ta*-[x x x x x (x)]
9 ⌜x x⌝ *ana* TI ZI-*ia ma-ḫ*[*ar*]-⌜*ku-nu*⌝ ⌜*kam*⌝-*sa*-[*ku* (x x)]
10 [Ḫ]UL *aš-qú-la-li ši-te-e ù* ⌜x x x⌝ [x x x x x]
11 [*u*]*s-ḫa be-lu-ú-a i-da-a a-na* [x x (x)]
12 *a-di-ra-ti-ia ana ḫa-di-e šur-ka* [x x]
13 UD-*mi i-dir-ti-ia nu-um-mi*-[*ra* (-*ni*)]
14 *i-da-ti-ia it-ta-ti-ia zu-uk-k*[*a-a* (-*ni*)]
15 *ḫi-da-a-ti ù ri-ša-a-ti* UD-*mi-šam* ⌜*id-na* ?⌝ [(x x)]
16 *ina qi-bi-ti-ku-nu* ḪUL-*šú-nu a-a i*[*ṭ*]-⌜*ḫa*⌝-[*a*]
17 *a-a iq-ri-ba a-a is-ni-qa a-a* ⌜*ik-šu*⌝-[*da-an-ni*]

---

18 ÉN 3-*šú* ŠID-*nu-ma* ⌜*uš*⌝-*ki*-[*en*]
19 *ana* IGI ^{d}UTU NÍG.NA ŠIM.LI GAR-*an mi*-⌜*iḫ*⌝-[*ḫa*]
⌜BAL⌝-[*qí*]
20 *ut-ni-en* NU IM DÙ-*uš* ḪUL ⌜x x x x x⌝
21 *ana* IGI ^{d}UTU GUB-*sú* [U]R$_5$.GIM DUG$_4$.[GA]

---

22 ^{d}UTU DI.KU$_5$ AN-*e u* KI-*t*[*im*]
23 AN-*e u* KI-*tum i-riš-šu*-[*ka*]

Reverse

1 [*er-ṣe-tum ù šá-m*]*a-mi kit-mu-su* IGI-[*ka*]
2 *a-w*[*i*]-⌜*lu-tum*⌝ ⌜*ma*⌝-[*l*]*a šu-ma na-bat ú-pa-qu k*[*a-a-ša*]
3 [ID]IM.MEŠ KUR.MEŠ ÍD.MEŠ ⌜ḪÉ⌝.GÁL *na-ši-a*-[*ka*]
4 *be-lí i-na na-pa-ḫi-ka* AN *u* KI *i-ḫal-lu-lu* [(-*ni*)]
5 *ma-lu-ú nam-ri-r*[*i*]
6 *tu-na-kar* ⌜*lum*⌝-[*n*]*am dum-qá* ⌜*ma*⌝-[*aš*]-⌜*ra*⌝-*a ta-šár-rak*
7 *aš-šum* ⌜ḪUL⌝ *ip-ri-ka* I[GI-*ka*] *ak-m*[*is* ?]
8 NU ⌜*pu*⌝-[*ḫ*]*i-ia* IG[I-*ka*] *uš-zi-i*[*z*]
9 *aš-šum* [Ḫ]UL-*i šu-uš-ḫu-ṭi qí-m*[*at*]-*su ú-šá-aš-ḫ*[*i-iṭ*]
10 IGI-*ka* ⌜*lum*⌝-*nam ad-din-šu a-a iṭ-ḫa-a a-a iq-r*[*i-ba*]
11 *a-a-ši* IGI-*ka a-a is-ni-qa* ḪUL *li-ni-ṭi*-[*ir*]
12 ⌜ḪUL⌝ [ÍD] *lim-ḫur-ma* IGI-*ka lu-bi - i*[*b*]
13 3-*šú* ⌜ŠID⌝-[*n*]*u-ma* NU *a-na* ÍD ŠUB-*d*[*i*]
14 *ana* ⌜EGIR⌝-*šú ul ip-pa - la - a*[*s*]

TRANSLATION

Obverse

1 [. . .]
2 [. . .]

3 [. . .] the goddess of the house [. . .]
4 He places a censer containing juniper resin at the door of his house. He says the following.

---

5 O god of the house, O goddess of the house [. . .]
6 You who make the seed to sprout [. . .]
7 You rejoiced and so we rejoiced [. . .]
8 (But now) you have given an omen that bodes unhappiness [. . .]
9 [. . .] for the well-being of my life, I kneel before you.
10 The devising of the evil brought on by the whirlwind(?) and [. . .]
11 Remove, O my lords, cast down to [. . .]
12 Grant that my sorrows turn to rejoicing [. . .]
13 Make bright my gloomy days.
14 Render my signs and portents propitious.
15 Give me happiness and rejoicing every day.
16 By your command may their evil not draw near,
17 Let it not approach, come nigh, nor reach me.

---

18 He recites the incantation three times and prostrates himself.
19 He places a censer containing juniper resin before Šamaš. He makes a libation of *miḫḫu*-beer.
20 He prays. He makes a clay figurine. He [. . .] the evil [. . .]
21 He sets it up in front of Šamaš. He says the following.

---

22 O Šamaš, judge of heaven and earth,
23 Heaven and earth rejoice in thee.

Reverse

1 Earth and sky kneel down before thee.
2 All men that have been called into being wait upon thee.
3 The springs of the mountains and the rivers bring thee abundance.
4 My lord, heaven and earth hum with activity when thou risest.
5 They are filled with brightness.
6 Thou removest evil, thou bestowest prosperity and wealth.
7 Because evil thwarts me, I have knelt before thee.
8 I have set up before thee a figurine that serves as my substitute.
9 In order to have the evil that afflicts me stripped away, I have had its (i.e. the figurine's) hair stripped off.

10 In thy presence I have transferred the evil to it. Let it (i.e. the evil) not draw near, let it not approach;

11 Let it not come nigh me in thy presence. Let the evil be taken away.

12 Let the river receive the evil so that I may become pure before thee.

13 He recites this three times and throws the figurine in a river.

14 He does not look behind him.

NOTES

Obverse

14 Note *it-ta-ti*, pl. of *ittu*, written syllabically in this SB text. Landsberger's statement that the pl. of *ittu*, meaning "omen," is, apart from the passages in NB royal inscriptions listed in *CAD* I/J 306b, "durchweg, soweit syllabisch geschrieben *i-da-a-tu*, ausnahmslos in SB" (*WO* 3, 70, n. 84), is to be corrected accordingly. This line also establishes the "reines Wortgeklingel" of *idāti ittāti* denied by Landsberger (*ibid.*).

Reverse

1 For the rare word-order *erṣetum u šamāmū*, cf. *ur-ti* KI-*tim u šá-ma-mi STC* 2 76:13.

4 *iḫallulu* – with *u* as its characteristic vowel, and so *ḫalālu* B of *CAD*, *ḫalālu* II of *AHw*.

9 Cf. *lu šu-uš-*⸢*ḫu*⸣*-ṭa lem-ni-tu-ú-a BBR* 26 iii 15 (reference from E. Reiner). *qí-m*[*at*]*-su*, as suggested by W. G. Lambert, seems preferable to *ki-š*[*ad*]*-su*, "its neck."

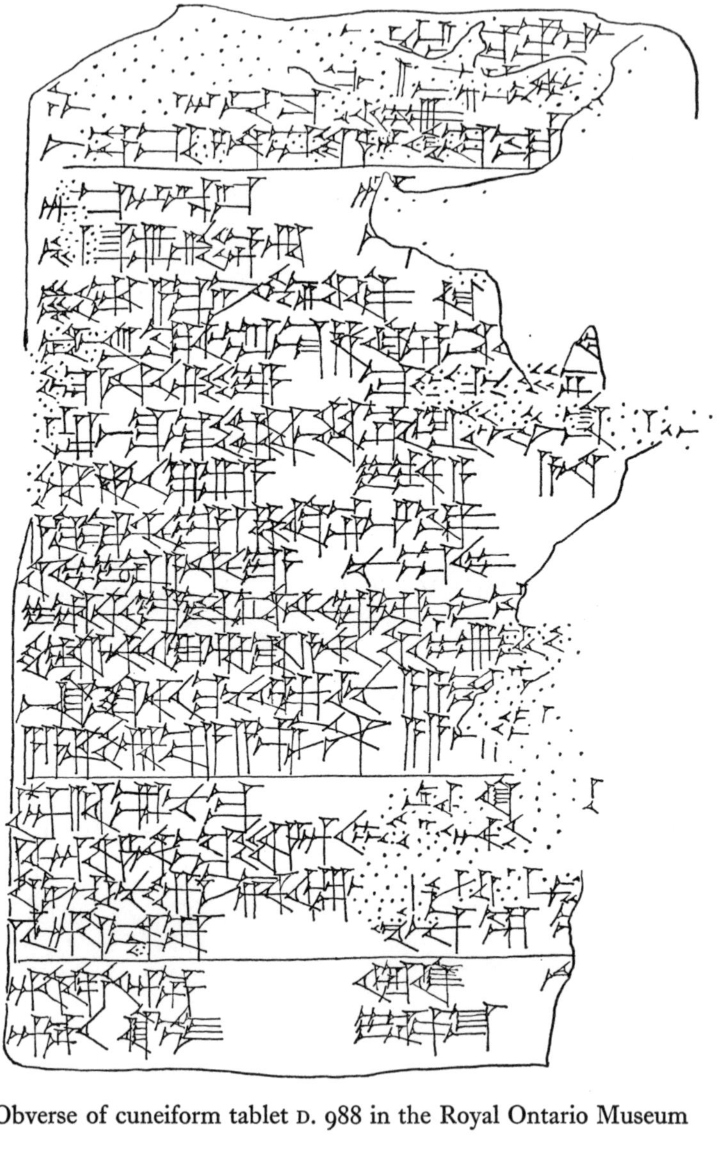

Obverse of cuneiform tablet D. 988 in the Royal Ontario Museum

Obverse of cuneiform tablet D. 988 in the Royal Ontario Museum
Dimensions of tablet $8\frac{1}{2}$ cm by 6 cm

Obverse, upper edge

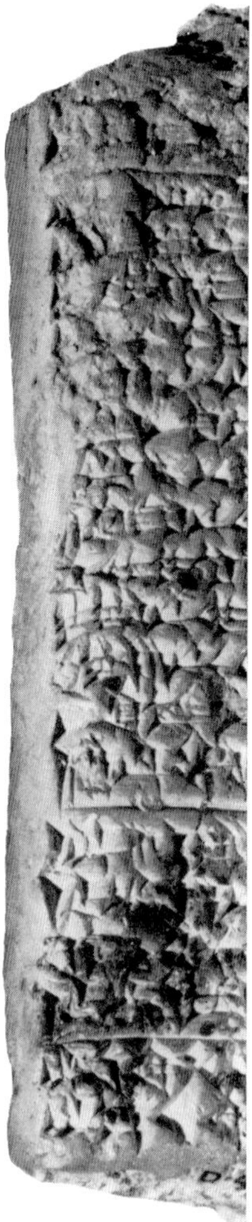

Obverse, left edge

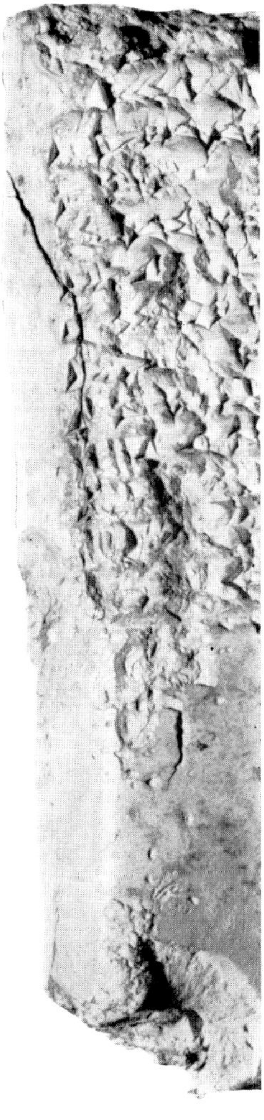

Reverse, upper edge

Reverse, left edge

Reverse of cuneiform tablet D. 988 in the Royal Ontario Museum

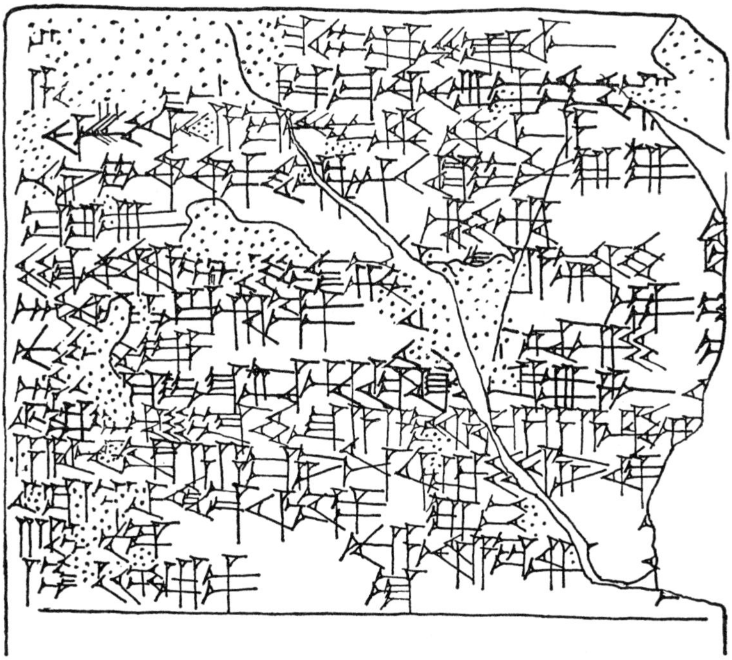

Reverse of cuneiform tablet D. 988

Metrical Analysis of Classical Hebrew Poetry

R. C. CULLEY

In spite of the fact that many capable scholars have turned their attention to the problem of the poetic structure of Classical Hebrew poetry, no agreement has been reached; in fact sharp differences of opinion have arisen. There are those who favour a theory, usually associated with the name of E. Sievers, which assumes a limited number of stressed syllables per line with great freedom as to the number of unstressed syllables permitted.[1] According to this proposal lines might have four, five, six, seven, or eight stresses. In direct contrast to this is a theory, advocated especially by S. Mowinckel, according to which the line consists of an alternation of stressed and unstressed syllables. This results in a higher number of stresses per line than the theory of Sievers. Then there are those who claim that a "word-metre" which takes the word as the unit to be counted best answers the characteristics of Hebrew poetry.[2] Furthermore, the suggestion has been made that more than one system may have been in use during the several hundred years of poetic composition in Hebrew.[3] "Word-metre" may have belonged

1 For discussion of the major theories, see any good introduction to the Old Testament, such as O. Eissfeldt, *Einleitung in das Alte Testament* (3rd ed. rev.; Tübingen: J. C. B. Mohr, 1964), pp. 75ff.; also S. Mowinckel, *The Psalms in Israel's Worship*, trans. D. R. Ap-Thomas (Oxford: Blackwell, 1962), vol. II, pp. 261–6, and Luis Alonso Schökel, *Estudios de Poética Hebrea* (Barcelona: Juan Flors, 1963), pp. 119–93.

2 H. Kosmala, "Form and Structure in Ancient Hebrew Poetry," *VT* 14 (1964), pp. 423–45. Although he does not use the term "word-metre," Kosmala takes the word or thought unit as the element which was counted in Ancient Hebrew poetry.

3 S. Segert, "Vorarbeiten zum hebräischen Metrik (I, II)," *Archiv Orientální*, 21 (1953), pp. 481–542, and also his "Problems of Hebrew Prosody," *Supplements to Vetus Testamentum*, 7 (1960), pp. 283–91.

to the earliest period, while the alternating stress system may have belonged to the latest stage. Still others hesitate to accept any of the theories which have been proposed so far, although they are willing to believe that some kind of metrical system was used.[4] Finally, a dissatisfaction with all theories has led some to suspect that metre played no role at all in the composition of Classical Hebrew.[5]

The very existence of such a wide range of opinion engenders a certain scepticism about the validity of any of the solutions offered so far. At the root of the matter lies the fact that we lack much of the information necessary to construct a theory of poetic structure which would be convincing enough to meet the approval of a very significant segment of informed opinion. In the first place, we are at a distinct disadvantage in having to rely on a text without being able to hear biblical poetry performed in its original setting. We do not know which texts were performed to music or what the music was like, and so we are unable to establish to what extent the texts may have been adjusted to the music, receiving a structure not clearly apparent in the texts themselves. It is also impossible to determine whether certain vowels were regularly elided in either sung or recited poetry. Similarly, other features relevant to metrical structure, yet not marked in our present text, cannot be identified. Furthermore, we do not know which texts were composed and transmitted orally or how such texts came to be written down. This information might be important for a discussion of poetic structure. For example, it is known that the poetic structure of oral poems composed to be sung may be distorted when they are put into writing because the singer is forced to recite slowly during dictation, thus losing his sense of the poetic form.[6]

Then too, the text of the Hebrew Bible which we now possess does not provide us with much of the information we would like to have. This text has been normalized in accordance with pronunciation at later stages of the development of the language and bears only traces of earlier stages of the language and variant dialects. Thus it is virtually impossible to establish all the ways in which older poems may have been modified during the course of transmission. It may have been that such poems were modernized by

4 See the comments of S. Gevirtz, *Patterns in the Early Poetry of Israel* (Studies in Ancient Oriental Civilization, 32; Chicago: University of Chicago Press, 1963), pp. 12–13.

5 See, for example, C. H. Gordon, *Ugaritic Manual* (Analecta Orientalia, 35; Rome: Pontificium Institutum Biblicum, 1955), p. 108, n. 1.

6 R. Austerlitz, *Ob-Ugric Metrics* (*FF Communications* 174, 1958), p. 101.

the substitution of new words and forms for old. Thinking specifically of historical grammar, we know that certain important changes in the structure of the language have occurred, such as dropping of final short vowels and a shift in stress. All such changes and modifications are the sort which may have had an effect on any metrical structure the poems may have had.

Precisely because we lack the kind of information just mentioned, it is not easy to evaluate metrical theories when they are proposed. It is as difficult to prove a theory wrong as it is to prove it right. We can do little more than express our scepticism by pointing out ways in which a given theory does not fit the text as neatly as we think it should.

But is there any other method of analysing poetic texts in Classical Hebrew which might prove useful in the present situation? It would appear that metrical theories produced so far have been arrived at by a combination of observing the text and testing possible hypotheses. The text has been examined for regularly recurring patterns, and then metrical schemes determined on the basis of this examination have been applied to the text to see how well they fit or even how they can be made to fit. However, in view of the varied results obtained by this method it would seem to be more profitable to search for a strictly descriptive approach in which certain features of the text are simply described in some systematic way. To be sure, a descriptive approach will not lead directly to a solution of the problem of Hebrew metre, but it may provide a way of discussing and comparing the poetic structure of poetic texts with which most could agree and upon which further discussion could be based. It is certainly true that scholars who are reluctant to be very explicit about the precise nature of Hebrew metre often simply give counts of stresses and syllables in the lines of poetry under consideration, which is itself a descriptive approach.[7] But can we not find a more thorough and systematic way of applying a descriptive method?

What is meant by a "descriptive" method should be clear. The term is well known from its use in linguistics. Such an approach for Hebrew poetry would involve describing a given text by measuring some of the characteristics relevant to metre, without introducing concepts like "feet" or "beats" in order to see if the text reflects thereby a shape or pattern which might be useful in a comparison

7 For example, D. N. Freedman, "Archaic Forms in Early Hebrew Poetry," *ZAW* 72 (1960), pp. 101–7.

with other texts analysed in the same way. That is to say, as few assumptions as possible are made about the text. Even the question of the existence of metre at all is held in suspension. A descriptive approach has in fact been used in the study of the poetry of other languages, quite often by linguists who have already found such a method helpful in the study of language. One example of a strictly descriptive approach being applied to a traditional oral poetry may be seen in a monograph by R. Austerlitz.[8]

Turning to the description of Classical Hebrew poetry, it is necessary first of all to establish which features relevant to metre might be measured or counted. Perhaps the first feature which springs to mind is stress. The theories of metre associated with the names of Sievers and Mowinckel are both concerned with the number of stresses in lines and cola, although each system arrives at a different estimate of the relevant stresses in these segments. Even though many would claim that metrical systems employed in Hebrew poetry would likely be accentual, there are certain disadvantages in making stress the unit to be counted. Some of these have already been mentioned. Unless the poetry concerned is carefully recorded during a performance in its original setting, an accurate description of the numbers and kinds of stress cannot be given. Nor does the masoretic tradition provide an unambiguous account of this. For example, there is the question of the kind of stress small particles might receive and whether this could vary and under what conditions. Another complicating factor is the likelihood of a shift in stress during the history of the language. It should also be recognized that, in texts which were sung, it is not always necessary for the stress in the music to coincide with the linguistic stress, since the text may be accommodated or adjusted to the melody.[9] Thus, while stress may be relevant for metrical analysis, there are considerable difficulties facing anyone attempting to produce a measurement of poetic structure based on a count of stress.

Another procedure which might reflect something of the poetic structure would be to count the number of words in lines and cola.[10]

8 *FF Communications* 174, 1958. This study suggested to me the possibility of a descriptive analysis of Hebrew poetry. An interesting collection of articles on metre may be found in Thomas H. Sebeok, ed., *Style in Language* (New York: John Wiley & Sons, 1960), especially the article by J. Lotz, "Metric Typology," pp. 135–48.

9 This is well expressed in Austerlitz, *Ob-Ugric Metrics*, pp. 124f. See also the comments of F. M. Cross, Jr. and D. N. Freedman, "The Blessing of Moses," *JBL* 67 (1948), pp. 191–210.

10 See above, n. 2.

Although such a count would provide a measurement of poetic structure, there are possible complications with this procedure as well. The fundamental problem is to decide what constitutes the word. Which of the small particles should be counted and which should not? Or, if "word" is to be understood as a thought unit, how are the boundaries of these thought units to be discerned? Decisions can be made on all these points, but the more subjective these decisions are, the less such an analysis merits the term "descriptive."

The last method of measuring to be mentioned is the counting of syllables. Even though the obvious lack of numerical regularity of syllables in lines and cola seems to rule out a syllable-counting metre, it has been recognized that a syllable count may be a useful clue to poetic structure.[11] But, as already pointed out, this sort of analysis faces problems since the masoretic text does not accurately reproduce the language of the biblical poets. Changes have occurred as the language developed which have had their effect on syllabic structure, such as the disappearance of final short vowels marking case and the syncope of certain vowels and consonants.[12] Another case in point would be the addition of anatyptic vowels to doubly closed monosyllables. Even if we were confident enough about our knowledge of historical grammar to reconstruct a text in the form of the language at the time of composition, uncertainties would still remain. For example, both oral poetry and traditional poetry which goes back to an oral tradition often preserve a mixture of old and new forms, words, and phrases.[13] Thus, a given text might bear the characteristics of more than one stage of the language so that a reconstruction might still be inaccurate. Finally, we have no way of knowing if the text was modified in singing or reciting by the elision of vowels thereby changing the syllabic content of a line.

Nevertheless, there are reasons for believing that counting syllables might still prove to be a useful means of investigation. In this respect, the most important feature of the syllable-counting method is that the number of syllables per colon is rather high in comparison with the number of stresses or words. A count of the number of syllables in a colon could therefore be used to make

11 Freedman, "Archaic Forms," pp. 101 and 107.

12 Z. S. Harris, *Development of Canaanite Dialects* (New Haven: American Oriental Society, 1939), provides a convenient inventory of these and other changes.

13 The writer's monograph *Oral Formulaic Language in the Biblical Psalms* (Toronto: University of Toronto Press, 1967), pp. 15–16, 99.

significant comparisons with the approximate counts of other cola and reveal relative differences and similarities in length. Such a procedure would seem much more feasible with the relatively high numbers of syllables per line and colon than with the much lower numbers of stresses or words. Even though the numbers of syllables counted in lines or cola would have to be considered to be approximations of what the numbers may have been originally, nonetheless the numbers of syllables obtained in the present text may still reveal the contour of an earlier poetic structure when larger groups of lines and cola are examined.

Once it is clear that the numbers of syllables counted in cola and lines are only to be considered approximate and not absolute figures, then it may be possible to use the masoretic text as a basis for counting without any reconstruction of the text in the light of our knowledge of historical grammar. Some may insist that we will come closer to the original form of the text by taking some cognizance of historical development, e.g. the removal of anatyptic vowels. This might prove to be a good procedure if agreement can be reached on the ways in which a text should be adjusted to conform with earlier stages of the language. However, it remains to be seen how great an advantage there would be in following such procedures, and so for the present investigation the masoretic text will be used as it stands.

Unfortunately, a decision to use the masoretic text as it stands does not resolve all difficulties. There is the problem of how to read the so-called medium *shewa*. Should this kind of *shewa* be considered vocal and thus be the nucleus of a syllable or should it be considered silent and thus be the marker of the closure of a syllable? Although many scholars have followed Sievers in taking the medium *shewa* as silent,[14] some, particularly Bergsträsser,[15] have raised sufficient objections to suggest that the issue is not clear. And so for the purposes of this investigation the so-called medium *shewa* will be taken as vocal. Admittedly, this is an arbitrary decision. But so was the previous decision to use the masoretic text. The intention of these arbitrary decisions is to set aside for the time being a number of very difficult problems so that the work

14 For example, Harris, *Development of Canaanite Dialects*, pp. 66f.; H. Bauer and P. Leander, *Historische Grammatik der hebräischen Sprache* (Halle: Niemeyer, 1922), pp. 209f.; W. Gesenius and E. Kautsch, *Hebrew Grammar* (2nd English ed. by A. E. Cowley; Oxford: Clarendon Press, 1910), pp. 51f.

15 G. Bergsträsser, *Hebräische Grammatik* (Leipzig: Vogel, 1918–29), vol. I, pp. 60ff. and 121ff.; also the comment in vol. II, p. 176.

of analysis may begin. Ordinarily this would be an irresponsible avoidance of important issues; but the justification in this case is that the figures produced will always be viewed as approximations, a certain latitude inevitably being allowed for changes which may have taken place due to language development or textual transmission. The real test of this method will come in the application of it to texts and in its ability to provide useful and significant information.

Before going on to the analysis of texts, one final matter must be considered. In order to count the syllables in lines and cola it is necessary first of all to establish clearly these divisions in the text. For much of biblical poetry this is not particularly difficult, since the lines and the cola into which lines are frequently divided are quite commonly marked off by the phenomenon usually called "parallelism." Furthermore, the ends of lines generally coincide with a major break in the syntactic structure, such as clause boundary. Very often the break within the line which divides it into cola is also marked by clause boundary. Since counting syllables in lines and cola is intended to be a strictly descriptive technique of measuring poetic structure, no count may be made where divisions into lines or cola are not evident from the text itself through the presence of parallelism or of relevant syntactic structure. This means, of course, that there may be parts of poems, or even whole poems, which cannot be analysed by means of a syllable count.

The following sections present the results of syllable counting when applied to various texts.

(*a*) *Psalm III*

The number of syllables per colon is:

vs. 1	8, 8	vs. 5	7, 8	vs. 9	7, 8, 7
2	8, 9	6	9, 9	10	8, 8, 9
3	7, 9	7	10, 8		
4	9, 7	8	8, 9		

The results may be stated in the following chart:

Number of syllables	7	8	9	10
Number of cola of each length	5	9	7	1

and summarized in the following way:

Range	7–10	(4)
Significant range	7–9	(3)
Most frequent length	8, then 9	

This summary shows that the range of possibilities in this psalm is from 7 to 10 syllables per colon. The following number in brackets indicates that this range includes four places on the ascending scale. The next line gives the range within which a significant number of cola fall. In this case a very high number of cola have 7, 8, or 9 syllables, giving a range of three places on the scale. The most frequent length is given in the last line of the summary as 8, and the following number indicates that the second most frequent length is 9 syllables.

(*b*) *Psalm 112*

The number of syllables per colon is:

vs. 1	9, 8	vs. 5	7, 9	vs. 9	8, 8, 7
2	9, 7	6	7, 9	10	7, 8, 9
3	7, 9	7	9, 9		
4	10, 8	8	7, 8		

Chart:	Syllables	7	8	9	10
	Cola	7	7	7	1

Summary:	Range	7–10	(4)
	Significant range	7–9	(3)
	Most frequent length	7, 8, and 9	

Psalms 111 and 112 are both quite short, although together they have forty-four cola. These cola are clearly marked by the acrostic structure of the psalms. The range and significant range and the same in each.

(*c*) *Job 6*

In the following, verses 2 and 10 have been omitted because there is some doubt about the division of the line into cola. In the other twenty-seven lines, there is no particular problem in dividing the lines into cola. Usually the break in the line is obvious from the parallel structure. In the few places where there appears to be no parallelism, there is a clause boundary in the middle of the line.

vs. 3	9, 7	vs. 9	10, 9	vs. 16	8, 8
4	8, 9, 10	11	7, 10	17	9, 10
5	9, 8	12	7, 6	18	9, 10
6	11, 9	13	7, 10	19	8, 9
7	7, 7	14	8, 8	20	5, 9
8	9, 8	15	9, 10	21	7, 8

vs. 22	8, 11	vs. 25	9, 8	vs. 28	9, 9
23	8, 9	26	9, 8	29	8, 7
24	9, 9	27	7, 7	30	8, 8

Chart:	Syllables	5	6	7	8	9	10	11
	A (1st colon in line)	1		6	8	10	1	1
	B (2nd colon in line)		1	4	8	8	5	1
	C (3rd colon in line)						1	
	Total	1	1	10	16	18	7	2

Summary:	Range	5–11	(7)
	Significant range	7–10	(4)
	Most frequent length	9, then 8	

(*d*) *Job 9*

Parallelism is once again common and so the division of the lines into cola is clear in most cases. Where the parallelism is not obvious, there is normally a clause boundary. In two places, verses 4 and 9, the division has been made at clause builder or phrase boundary. In view of the way all the other lines appear to be divided, it seems likely that these verses should also be divided into two cola. Some might insist that such verses should be omitted from a descriptive analysis, but the risk of including them here is small. They can easily be subtracted from the results if necessary. Verse 21 has been omitted.

vs. 2	7, 8	vs. 13	7, 10	vs. 25	8, 8
3	7, 11	14	9, 8	26	9, 9
4	8, 8	15	10, 8	27	8, 10
5	10, 8	16	9, 10	28	8, 9
6	9, 9	17	10, 8	29	5, 7
7	10, 8	18	9, 9	30	9, 9
8	8, 8	19	7, 10	31	8, 8
9	5, 9	20	8, 8	32	10, 7
10	9, 8	22	8, 8	33	7, 8
11	10, 9	23	6, 8	34	7, 10
12	8, 9	24	9, 9	35	10, 9

Chart:	Syllables	5	6	7	8	9	10	11
	A	2	1	6	9	8	7	
	B			2	15	10	5	1
	C		1					
	Total	2	2	8	24	18	12	1

Summary:	Range	5–11	(7)
	Significant range	7–10	(4)
	Most frequent length	8, then 9	

(*e*) *Numbers 23:710, 18–24 and 24:3–9, 15–18*

These sections contain thirty-five lines. The first line in verse 10 has been omitted. Parallelism is common. Where this does not indicate the division of the line, clause boundary has been taken as the marker of the break between cola.

Numbers 23

vs. 7	8, 10, 8, 9	vs. 18	6, 10	vs. 22	8, 7
8	7, 9	19	6, 8, 9, 9	23	8, 8, 9, 9
9	8, 9, 7, 8	20	7, 9	24	7, 7, 8, 7
10	8, 10	21	9, 10, 7, 7		

Numbers 24

vs. 3	8, 11	vs. 15	8, 11	vs. 18	8, 11, 8
4	8, 10, 8	16	8, 7, 8, 8		
9	7, 9, 7, 7	17	7, 8, 8, 8, 8, 7		

Chart:

Syllables	5	6	7	8	9	10	11
A		3	10	17	3	2	
B			10	11	7	4	3
C	1			2			
Total	1	3	20	30	10	6	3

Summary:

Range	5–11	(7)
Significant range	7–10	(4)
Most frequent length	8, then 7	

(*f*) *Psalm 2*

In this psalm, the last colon of verse 11 has not been counted because the text is obscure. The division of verse 8 might be challenged. Here it has been taken as a line with three cola on the basis of a clause boundary after the second word and the repetition in the last three words of what immediately precedes.

vs. 1	7, 7	vs. 5	10, 10	vs. 9	8, 9
2	9, 9, 8	6	8, 6	10	9, 9
3	10, 11	7	8, 8, 8	11	9
4	8, 7	8	5, 11, 10	12	10, 8, 7

Chart:

Syllables	5	6	7	8	9	10	11
A	1		1	4	3	3	
B		1	2	2	3	1	2
C			1	2		1	
Total	1	1	4	8	6	5	2

Summary: Range 5–11 (7)
Significant range 7–10 (4)
Most frequent length 8, then 9

(g) Psalm 78

Parallelism is very frequent. Verse 19 and the first line of verse 38 have been omitted. In a very few cases clause builder or phrase boundary has been accepted as the division between cola.

Chart:

Syllables	6	7	8	9	10	11	12	13	14
A	2	7	24	25	12	4	2	1	8
B	4	10	23	25	12	3			
C				3					1
Total	6	17	47	53	24	7	2	1	1

Summary: Range 6–14 (9)
Significant range 7–10 (4)
Most frequent length 9, then 8

Note that 100 out of 158 cola are either 8 or 9 syllables long.

(h) Psalm 96

Chart:

Syllables	7	8	9	10	11	12	13
A	3	1	3	3	2	1	1
B	1	5	5	1	1	1	
C		1					
Total	4	7	8	4	3	2	1

Summary: Range 7–13
Most frequent length 9, then 8

The significant range might be said to be 7–10, but since there are about the same number of lines with 10, 11, 12, and 13 syllables it would not be meaningful to make a division anywhere.

At this point a few remarks may be made about the examples (*a*) to (*h*). The significant range is around 7 to 10. The most frequent length is approximately 8. In other words these examples show roughly the same configuration in their charts and summaries.

(i) Psalm 89

Vss. 21–46

Chart:

Syllables	6	7	8	9	10
A	2	7	9	7	2
B		3	14	7	3
Total	2	10	23	14	5

Summary: Range 6–10 (5)
Significant range 7–9 (3)
Most frequent length 8

This summary is much the same as in the preceding examples, but verses 1–19 of the same psalm produce a different set of figures. Verse 20 has been omitted.

Vss. 1–19

Chart:

Syllables	7	8	9	10	11	12	13	14
A	1	2	4	6	4	1		
B		1	1	4	5	3	3	1
Total	1	3	5	10	9	4	3	1

Summary: Range 7–14 (8)
Most frequent length 10, then 11

A significant range is not clearly discernible here.

While verses 21–46 of Psalm 89 produce a summary similar to examples (*a*) to (*h*), verses 1–19 of the same psalm produce a summary similar to the following examples.

(*j*) *Psalm 74*

Verses 5, 11, and 20 are omitted.

Chart:

Syllables	6	7	8	9	10	11	12	13	14
A	1		3	3	6	4	1	1	1
B		1	1	2	4	7	5		
C		1							
Total	1	2	4	5	10	11	6	1	1

Summary: Range 6–14 (9)
Most frequent length 10, then 11

(*k*) *Psalm 17*

Verse 10 is omitted.

Chart:

Syllables	8	9	10	11	12	13	14	15
A	1	2	6	2	1	2		1
B		1	5	6	1	1		1
Total	1	3	11	8	2	3		2

Summary: Range 8–15 (8)
Most frequent length 10, then 11

(l) Psalm 9:2–21

Verse 7 is omitted.

Chart:

Syllables	7	8	9	10	11	12	13	14	15
A	1	5	3	7		1	1		
B	1	1	7	6		2			1
Total	2	6	10	13		3	1		1

Summary:

Range	7–15	(9)
Significant range	8–10	(3)
Most frequent length	10, then 9	

There are gaps in the table, but a preference is still shown for 9 or 10 syllables.

(m) Psalm 41

Verses 3 and 7 are omitted.

Chart:

Syllables	7	8	9	10	11	12	13	14
A	1	1	1	4	2		1	1
B	1	1	3	4	1	1		
Total	2	2	4	8	3	1	1	1

Summary:

Range	7–14	(8)
Most frequent length	10	

The last few examples, the last part of (*i*) and (*j*) to (*m*), are similar in that they have a range of about 7 to 15 syllables and the most frequent length is approximately 10 syllables.

All the examples given so far, then, fall into two groupings: (*a*) to (*h*) along with the first part of (*i*), which have approximately 8 syllables as the most frequent length, and (*j*) to (*m*) along with the last part of (*i*), which have approximately 10 syllables as the most frequent length.

All the charts and summaries of the above examples have been based on the number of syllables in the colon. Three factors suggested that the colon could be taken as a unit in these examples: the acrostic structure of Psalms 111 and 112; the high incidence of parallelism pointing to a clear break in the line, the break frequently being indicated by the syntactic structure as well; and the existence of long lines which could be divided into three cola. The preceding examples can also be analysed on the basis of the number of syllables in the line. Although not all the examples produce results which can be stated in a meaningful summary, examples (*c*), (*d*), (*e*), and (*g*) show a range of anywhere from 12 to 21 syllables per line with the most frequent length being about 16 or 17 syllables. While analysis on the basis of cola seemed the most appropriate for examples (*a*) to (*m*), it need not be the best procedure to follow in all cases. The structure of the lines must give the clue. Where there is no division in the lines clearly and regularly marked by the poetic or syntactic structure, it would be preferable to begin by counting the syllables in the line. The following examples are of this sort.

(*n*) *Psalm 119*

The lines are clearly marked by the acrostic structure of the poem, but parallelism is not so common as to make a division of the lines into cola an easy matter. Thus, the following chart and summary are measurements of the lines. Verses 128 and 137 are omitted, leaving a total of 174 lines.

Chart:	Syllables	13	14	15	16	17	18	19	20	21	22	23	24
	Lines	8	11	23	30	37	31	12	14	5	1	1	1

Summary:	Range	13–24 (12)
	Significant range	15–18 (4)
	Most frequent length	17, then 18, then 16

A similar pattern emerges here with lines as previously with cola. There is a fairly wide range of possibilities and a narrower range of significant occurrences. Of 174 lines, 121 are 15, 16, 17, or 18 syllables long. The most frequent length of line is 17 syllables, and moving from this point on the chart in either direction the numbers decrease.

While parallelism is not really common in this psalm, the line consists of two clauses in a large majority of cases so that there is a clause boundary which seems to mark a division of the line into two cola. The few examples of parallelism which do occur seem to support the assumption of a division in the lines. Thus it may be interesting to include the results of a syllable count of the twofold division of the line. In a few cases, where no clear parallelism or clause boundary exists, the verse has been divided at a phrase boundary. Several verses have been omitted because they contain no clues as to how they might be divided. These verses are 6, 14, 18, 20, 44, 46, 48, 52, 57, 62, 65, 76, 112, 125, 128, 132, 137, 145, 149, and 176. This leaves a total of 156 lines. It should be emphasized that the following chart and summaries are tentative and offered for information rather than for evidence. Psalm 119 is different from the examples offered so far in that parallelism is less frequent and there are no lines which could be considered as tricola.

Chart:

Syllables	4	5	6	7	8	9	10	11	12	13
A		1	8	14	40	38	29	17	7	2
B	1	8	13	32	43	38	16	4	1	
Total	1	9	21	46	83	76	45	21	8	2

Summary:

		A	B
Range	4–13 (10)	5–13 (9)	4–12 (9)
Significant range	7–10 (4)	8–10 (3)	7–9 (3)
Most frequent length	8, then 9	8, then 9, then 10	8, then 9, then 7

The summary of all the line divisions may be compared with the summaries of examples (*a*) to (*h*) above. It has the same general pattern. However, a comparison of the summaries of A and B shows a slight but interesting difference. In both, the most common length of colon is approximately 8 or 9 syllables, but a much larger number in A consist of 10 syllables and in B of 7 syllables. It would be premature to draw any conclusions, but it is worth noting that this analysis shows that more of B are short than of A. It is difficult to say at this point whether such a slight difference is significant when dealing with numbers which can only be taken as approximations.

(*o*) *Threni 1*

This poem has a similar structure to Psalm 119 in that a division in the line is not always clearly marked and there appear to be no lines which could be composed of three cola. The count of syllables in the lines will be given first.

Chart:

Syllables	10	11	12	13	14	15	16	17	18
Lines	2	9	10	20	8	10	4	3	1

Summary:

Range	10–18 (9)
Significant range	11–15 (5)
Most frequent length	13

The summary is significantly different from that of the lines in Psalm 119 at all levels.

If the lines are divided into two parts, the following chart may be drawn up. The division has been made on the basis of parallelism where it occurs, clause boundary, and clause builder or phrase boundary. These results must also be considered tentative since it has been assumed in a number of lines that the boundary between clause builders could be taken as a division point in the line.

The following lines have been omitted from consideration because the division is not indicated in any clear way by the text itself: the first line in vs. 1; the first and third lines in vs. 3; the first and fourth lines in vs. 7; the second and third lines in vs. 10; the first line in vs. 13; the third line in vs. 14; and the first line in vs. 15.

Chart:	Syllables	4	5	6	7	8	9	10	11
	A		5	8	20	13	4	5	1
	B	4	19	19	6	7	1		

		A		B	
Summary:	Range	5–11	(7)	4–9	(6)
	Significant range	7–8	(2)	5–6	(2)
	Most frequent length	7, then 8		5 and 6	

If there is, in fact, some kind of pause or break in the lines of this poem, the chart and summary suggest a significant difference in the average length of the A and the B cola, the B tending to be shorter.

These examples will be sufficient to illustrate the method and to make an evaluation of it possible. In the first place, the selections of poetry given in the examples yield results which produce significant patterns when presented in charts and summaries. Taking the number of syllables in cola and lines to represent the approximate length of these units, a common pattern is seen in all the results. Even though a fairly wide range of different lengths is usually found in a given selection, most cola or lines fall somewhere around the middle of the range. For most of the examples it was possible to draw up a three-part summary. Within a fairly wide total range, a significant range may be seen into which most cola or lines fall. Similarly, within the significant range, one or two lengths can be identified as the most frequent. This length or these lengths might be designated as the "typical" length of cola or lines in a given poem. This pattern suggests that restrictions have been imposed upon the poetic structure, in that there appear to be limits set on the length of line and colon possible, and in addition the lines and cola tend toward a typical length. Although such patterns seem to suggest a metrical structure of some sort, it would be better not to speculate further on this subject until more poetry has been analysed. In any case, the usefulness of this kind of syllable count does not depend on its ability to divulge the precise metrical structure of texts. It will be sufficient if the method brings to light something of the poetic structure and permits some distinctions to be made within the corpus of Classical Hebrew poetry.

A study of the examples reveals, as already mentioned, that groupings can be discerned. The summaries of examples (*a*) to (*h*) are very similar, and so these might form one group with a typical length of approximately 8 or 9 syllables per colon. Then too, examples (*j*) to (*m*) might form another group with a typical length of about 10 syllables per colon. The final examples (*n*) and (*o*) are different from the others, and so were analysed on the basis of the length of line. While the summary of (*n*) was similar to the analysis of the lines of (*c*), (*d*), (*e*), and (*g*) already mentioned, the results for (*o*) were different, having lower figures in all three parts of the summary. For the sake of interest, a tentative division of the lines was attempted. A very slight tendency was seen in (*n*) for the second part of the line to be shorter than the first. Because the tendency was very slight, this may or may not be significant. However, in (*o*) this tendency was marked and likely reflects the poetic structure. The existence of the groupings and distinctions just mentioned strongly suggests that the method of syllable-counting will be useful, especially since these results have been obtained without adopting any particular stand on the problem of metre.

If the method proves acceptable, the rest of biblical poetry should be analysed, in so far as it lends itself to analysis. It is clear that poetry in which the colon or line structure is not clear cannot be analysed, and there may be a considerable amount of poetry in this category. It may then be seen what other poems fall into the groups described above and what new groups must be formed. It may also be noted what poems do not have similarities with any others or, perhaps, do not even display a significant pattern themselves. Then the implications of all these results might be pursued.

An Old Kingdom Relief of a Fan-bearer in the Royal Ontario Museum

DONALD B. REDFORD

The fragment of Old Kingdom relief discussed here comes from the excavations of the Metropolitan Museum of Art at Lisht,[1] and is at present to be found in the Royal Ontario Museum in Toronto.[2] The greatest width of the piece is 40 cm., the distance from crown to chin of the human figure being 4.8 cm. Apart from the flesh, coloured reddish-brown, and the wig, coloured black, no trace of pigment has survived. The scene depicts a fan-bearer in striated head-dress, bearing his long-handled fan across his left shoulder as he strides (?) to the right. The fragment preserved shows only the upper part of his body, his right forearm, kilt, and legs having been broken away. Behind him marched another fan-bearer, only part of whose fan is now preserved. Partly lost on the right is a *šmʿ*-sign, beneath which appears the left part of a *sꜣ*-sign. Above the entire scene a band of stars forms a border. Parts of only two stars are preserved, and these are above the human figures. To judge from the example on the left, the better preserved of the two, each was five-pointed

1 For bibliography, see B. Porter and R. Moss, *Topographical Bibliography of Ancient Egyptian Hieroglyphic Texts, Reliefs and Paintings* (7 vols.; Oxford, 1927–60), IV, pp. 77ff.

2 Acc. no. 958.49.2. It was published by Miss W. Needler in the *Annual of the Art and Archaelogy Division of the Royal Ontario Museum*, 1959, pp. 35f. I take this opportunity to thank Miss Needler for allowing me to study this relief, and for her criticism and suggestions.

and had a small circular centre point.[3] That the star band extended originally over the hieroglyphs as well is indicated by the straight edge of the break which continues the lower edge of the border.

It will scarcely be doubted that the fragment comes from a royal relief. The use of stars in rows as borders, or in ceiling decoration, was restricted to royalty in the Old Kingdom, although later this restriction was abolished.[4] The excellent craftsmanship reflected in the delicacy of the relief also points to the royal workshops. The very size of the scene when reconstructed (see below) – the fan-bearer was probably about 35 cm. tall, and he was a figure of lesser importance! – militates strongly in favour of a provenance in a royal temple. The reliefs from Abu Gurob and Abu Sir clinch the matter. Here in the reliefs from the Sun-temple[5] and the Pyramid-temple of Neuserre[6] fan-bearers are shown, always in close proximity to the king, frequently marching behind his palanquin in pairs.[7]

In view of these scenes it seems altogether likely that our piece is but a fragment from the upper left-hand corner of a larger scene in which the figure of a king, perhaps in a palanquin, was shown being carried in the midst of his courtiers to a state ceremony. The two fan-bearers would have appeared on an upper register just behind his head. Since in most of the examples of this type of scene the king's figure is at least twice as tall as those of his servants, in the present relief the king must have been *ca.* 70–80 cm. in height; and to the writer this seems a conservative estimate. If our reconstruction is correct, then the star band which runs across the fragment must have formed the top border of the entire scene, and

3 Other examples of stars from Old Kingdom reliefs are: J.-P. Lauer, *La Pyramide à degrés* (4 vols.; Cairo, 1935–59), I, p. 39, fig. 21; H. Schaeffer, *Mitt. Kairo* 4 (1933), p. 16, Abb. 18; G. A. Reisner and W. S. Smith, *A History of the Giza Necropolis*, II (Cambridge, Mass., 1955), fig. 7; L. Borchardt, *Das Grabdenkmal des Königs Saꜣhureʿ* (3 vols.; Leipzig, 1910–13), I, p. 49, fig. 51; *idem*, *Das Grabdenkmal des Königs Nefer-ir-keꜣ-reʿ* (Leipzig, 1909), p. 30, fig. 32; *idem*, *Das Grabdenkmal des Königs Ne-user-reʿ* (Leipzig, 1907), p. 59, fig. 40; G. Jéquier, *Le Monument funéraire de Pepi II* (3 vols., Cairo, 1936–40), *passim*; C. M. Firth and B. Gunn, *Teti Pyramid Cemeteries* (Cairo, 1926), pl. 57.

4 W. S. Smith, *A History of Egyptian Sculpture and Painting in the Old Kingdom* (Boston, 1949), p. 241.

5 W. Von Bissing and H. Kees, *Das Re-Heiligtum des Königs Ne-woser-re* (*Rathures*) (3 vols.; Leipzig, 1905–28), II, pls. 16:39, 17:42, 18:44c, 19:44a, 22:52.

6 Borchardt, *Ne-user-reʿ*, p. 85, fig. 62c.

7 *Re-Heiligtum*, pls. 16:39, 17:42, 19:45b. For examples from the Late Period, see E. Naville, *The Festival Hall of Osorkon II in the Great Temple of Bubastis* (London, 1892), pl. 25, and Sir W. M. F. Petrie, *The Palace of Apries* (*Memphis II*) (London, 1909), pl. 3.

not just the line of demarcation between one register and another.[8] Which ceremony the king was shown proceeding to is difficult to say; but on the analogy of the Fifth Dynasty reliefs already cited, it may well have been one of the rites of the *sd*-festival.

To the right of the fan-bearers are parts of two hieroglyphs, viz. the flowering sedge[9] and the looped cord.[10] The former stands on a flat, ovoid object, very slightly left of centre. The two sprouting stalks on the left (all that are preserved) have five little ovate leaflets. The stalks all coalesce at the bottom of the plant, so that the vertical groove which indicates their separation does not extend to the base.

Early examples of the sedge (into the Fourth Dynasty) represent the leaflets almost as drops of dew, and then only on the upper surface of the branching stalks.[11] The slenderness and delicacy of the Fifth Dynasty examples from royal reliefs are worth noting. Though the leaflets are often ovate like ours, their grouping is different,[12] and they are much smaller.[13] Private examples from the Fifth and Sixth Dynasty are carelessly executed.[14]

The lower sign shows the left part of the horizontal cord, and in part two of the subsidiary loops. The detail of the twisted strands is carefully shown, but it is not clear whether the subsidiary loops are attached to the main cord, or whether they pass beneath it. It is interesting to note that the subsidiary loop, which is best preserved, is slightly larger than the horizontal (main) loop. In the stela of Neter-aperef from the reign of Sneferu or Khufu, three looped cord signs occur with carefully carved detail like ours, but the subsidiary loops are much smaller than the horizontal.[15] The *sꜣ*-sign shows great variety in the number of pairs of subsidiary loops; we may cite the example of Neter-aperef with three loops,[16] Rahotpe

8 Star bands, of course, do not always occur at the extreme top of a scene; cf. *Re-Heiligtum*, pl. 8b. But in the scenes in which the king is shown in his palanquin together with fan-bearers, they invariably seem to.

9 Sir A. H. Gardiner, *Egyptian Grammar* (3rd ed.; Oxford, 1960), Sign List, M26.

10 *Ibid.*, V16.

11 H. O. Lange and M. Hirmer, *Egypt* (London, 1956), pl. 18; W. S. Smith, *The Art and Architecture of Ancient Egypt* (Harmondsworth, 1958), pl. 39a; R. Lepsius, *Denkmaeler aus Aegypten und Nubien*, II (Berlin, 1859), pls. 3, 4, 7; Sir W. M. F. Petrie *et al.*, *Medum* (London, 1892), pl. 13.

12 Borchardt, *Nefer-ir-keꜣ-reʿ*, p. 29, fig. 29; *idem*, *Saꜣhureʿ*, p. 45, pl. 10.

13 *Idem*, *Ne-user-reʿ*, pl. 14.

14 N. de G. Davies, *The Mastaba of Ptahhetep and Akhethetep* (2 vols.; London, 1900–1), I, pl. 10:176, 180, 182; M. A. Murray, *Saqqara Mastabas*, I (London, 1905), pl. 12, 39:49.

15 A. Fakhry, *ASAE* 52 (1954), pl. 21.

16 *Ibid.*

with three and four,[17] Khufu with five,[18] and others of Fourth Dynasty date with as many as seven![19] Unfortunately there is no indication as to how many subsidiary loops our sign contained. If ours possessed even three subsidiary pairs, the over-all length of the sign would cause it to extend far to the right of the sedge.

If, as we have suggested, the large figure of a king is to be restored at the lower right, the purport of at least one of the signs becomes clear. The *sꜣ*-sign belongs to the common wish *sꜣ ʿnḫ ḥꜣ.f*, "may protection and life surround him,"[20] written vertically behind the king. In that case the *šmʿ*-sign must belong to a different inscription. but it is difficult to restore it. A common motif in Old Kingdom reliefs which depict royalty is the falcon, with wings outspread, hovering over the king.[21] And in such scenes the falcon is often accompanied by the epithet *ḫnty ỉtrty Šmʿ*, "foremost one of the row of Upper Egypt(ian shrines)."[22] It is with some diffidence that I propose to restore this phrase in the fragment, together with a falcon farther to the right, fluttering above the king. The principal objection to such a reconstruction is that there does not seem to be enough space between the star border at the top and the point beneath at which the crown of the king's head would appear. The fact that royal reliefs do occur, however, in which fan-bearers beneath a star border are preceded by the falcon[23] lends support to the restoration here suggested; and it does not seem impossible that a small falcon was fitted into the space available.

The wig worn by the fan-bearer is of the long, striated type, so common in the Old Kingdom and later, down to the Saite Period. It consisted of a number of strands of hair,[24] joined at a central axis which lay along the centre of the skull.[25] The length varied from an

17 Petrie *et al.*, *Medum*, pl. 13 (upper right and lower left).

18 Sir A. H. Gardiner *et al.*, *The Inscriptions of Sinai* (2 parts; London, 1952–55), I, pl. 3.

19 K. Sethe, W. Helck, and others, *Urkunden des ägyptischen Altertums* (Leipzig, 1906–), I, 14:12.

20 A. Erman and H. Grapow, *Wörterbuch der ägyptischen Sprache* (5 vols., with reference vols.; Leipzig and Berlin, 1926–55), III, 414:20.

21 Cf., for example, the famous scene from the Step-Pyramid complex : Lange and Hirmer, *Egypt*, pl. 15.

22 Jéquier, *Monument funéraire*, II, pls. 46, 50, 51, 61 (restored). For a discussion of the expression, see Sir A. H. Gardiner, *JEA* 30 (1944), pp. 26ff.

23 Cf. Firth and Gunn, *Teti Pyramid Cemeteries*, pl. 57:1, 7. I am indebted to Miss Needler for this reference.

24 I.e. horse hair, human hair, or vegetable fibre : A. Lucas, *ASAE* 30 (1930), pp. 191ff.; on the subject of wigs see also E. A. Eisa, *ASAE* 48 (1948), pp. 9ff.

25 W. C. Hayes, *The Scepter of Egypt* (2 vols.; Cambridge, Mass., 1958), I, fig. 62 and p. 108.

inch or two below the ear to well below the shoulder.[26] When treated with liquid beeswax, which was then allowed to harden, and padded with vegetable fibre, the wig could be shaped in a variety of ways.[27] Hence the often bewildering number of shapes we see in sculpture and relief. Sometimes this long wig is depicted with two or more horizontal "bands" encircling (?) it at the lower end near the shoulder.[28] The purpose would almost appear to be to hold the loose strands of hair together; but it is probable that this was only a conventional way of representing the shorter length of two overlying layers of strands.[29]

The wig in the ROM relief consists of sixteen visible strands (not waved), the grooves between them being cut with boldness and care. The grooves are relatively deep, and the strands between rounded. In the later Old Kingdom there was a tendency to carve striated head-dresses with flat surfaces between the grooves.[30] The closest analogies to the present example come from the Fourth and early Fifth Dynasties.[31]

The most interesting feature of the relief is the fan. It is a large object in the shape of a lily-pad, with a long handle connected to it by means of a ball and socket. At the moment the fan is not in use. It is being held in readiness by its bearer for the time when the sovereign, or perhaps traditional procedure, should demand a cooling breeze and some shade for the royal pate.

To call the object a fan at this point may seem premature. Was it intended to waft air, or to provide protection from the heat? Or could the same object fulfil both functions? The most common royal sunshade (justly so-called) depicted on monuments of the New Kingdom is the *bht*.[32] It is seen, often in pairs or groups of

26 Very long wigs of this type, unless we have mistaken natural hair, were worn by the king and high officials in Protodynastic times: cf. Sir W. M. F. Petrie, *The Royal Tombs of the First Dynasty* (London, 1900), pl. 10:14; J. E. Quibell, *Hieraconpolis*, (2 vols.; London, 1901–2), I, pl. 29.

27 A. Lucas, *Ancient Egyptian Materials and Industries* (3rd ed.; London, 1948), pp. 41ff.

28 Cf. the wig of Redynes (Smith, *A History of Egyptian Sculpture and Painting*, pl. 57c).

29 J. Capart and M. Werbrouck, *Memphis à l'ombre des pyramides* (Brussels, 1930), p. 265, fig. 248.

30 Cf. Smith, *A History of Egyptian Sculpture and Painting*, pl. 54b; P. Duell, *The Mastaba of Mereruka* (2 vols.; Chicago, 1938), II, pl. 184.

31 Petrie *et al.*, *Meydum and Memphis III* (London, 1910), pl. 20:6; Smith, *A History of Egyptian Sculpture and Painting*, pls. 39, 40e, 41a, 42a, 53a; Lepsius, *Denkmaeler*, III, pl. 121a; W. Wreszinski, *Atlas zur altaegyptischen Kulturgeschichte*, III (Leipzig, 1938), Taf. 104, 337.

32 *Wörterbuch*, I, 467:3–6. Seldom used by non-royalty; cf. Lange and Hirmer,

three, shading the king when he goes abroad in his palanquin,[33] while he is riding in his chariot,[34] or when he is simply on foot.[35] The same service is accorded the statues of deceased kings and the sacred barques of the gods. Here the king is often shown as the fan-bearer of the god, wielding the sunshade before or behind the barque.[36] Sometimes the shade is attached to the vessel, either at prow or stern.[37] Even if not in use at the moment the scene commemorates, the *bht*-shades are shown held in readiness by members of the royal entourage.[38] So close a connection was thought to exist between this type of royal sunshade and the magical power of protection afforded by the king that the shape of the *bht* was imitated by the military standard called *sryt*.[39] That the latter was itself held in awe, and perhaps even worshipped, is graphically illustrated by the scene from Amarna which shows several *sryt* standards upon altars of their own.[40]

The *bht*-shade consisted of a semi-circle of ostrich-plumes set in a base of ivory or metal.[41] In the more detailed representations, the individual feathers may even be counted. Thus three sunshades from the time of Ramses IV from Abd el-Qurna show 33, 31, and 17 feathers respectively.[42] Two empty stocks from Tutankhamun's tomb at one time contained 48 and 42 feathers respectively.[43] The

---

Egypt, pl. 164 (below), and Nina M. Davies and Sir A. H. Gardiner, *Ancient Egyptian Paintings* (Chicago, 1936), pl. 73.

33 N. de G. Davies, *The Tomb of Huy* (EES Theban Tomb Series, IV; London, 1930), pls. 27 and 29; *idem, The Rock Tombs of El-Amarna* (EEF Archaeological Survey of Egypt, Memoirs 13 to 18; London, 1903–8), III, pl. 13; Lepsius, *Denkmaeler*, III, pl. 121a; Wreszinski, *Atlas*, I, pl. 173.

34 Smith, *The Art and Architecture of Ancient Egypt*, pl. 142; Lepsius, *Denkmaeler*, II, pls. 127a, 130a.

35 N. de G. Davies, *The Tomb of Menkheperrasonb, Amenmose and Another* (EES, Theban Tomb Series, V; London, 1933), pls. 3, 16; *idem, El-Amarna*, VI, pl. 3; Gardiner *et al.*, *The Inscriptions of Sinai*, I, pl. 58:179; Naville, *The Festival Hall of Osorkon II*, pl. 25; J. D. S. Pendlebury, T. E. Peet, and others, *The City of Akhenaten* (3 vols.; London, 1923–51), III, pl. 70:10.

36 Černý, *BIFAO* 27 (1927), p. 187, fig. 13; Lepsius, *Denkmaeler*, III, pls. 138a, 180a, 189b, 235; A. Mariette, *Abydos* (2 vols.; Paris, 1869–80), I, pp. 63, 70f.; Sir W. M. F. Petrie, *Koptos* (London, 1896), pl. 19; J. Vandier, *Deux tombes ramessides à Gournet-Mourrai* (*MIFAO* 87), pl. 6:2, 10; Wreszinski, *Atlas*, I, pl. 119.

37 Lepsius, *Denkmaeler*, III, pl. 173a.

38 Davies, *El-Amarna*, I, pls. 20, 30; II, pls. 5, 17, 18.

39 H. Kees, *Der Opfertanz der ägyptischen Königs* (Leipzig, 1912), p. 127; R. O. Faulner, *JEA* 27 (1941), pp. 12f.

40 Davies, *El-Amarna*, VI, pl. 20 and p. 13; pl. 30 and p. 23.

41 Lucas, *Ancient Egyptian Materials*, p. 40.

42 Lepsius, *Denkmaeler*, III, pl. 235; cf. also Wegner, *Mitt. Kairo* 4 (1933), pls. 11b, 12b.

43 H. Carter, *The Tomb of Tut-ankh-amen* (3 vols.; London, 1923–33), III, p. 133.

papyrus mentions plants and blossoms in connection with the *bht*.[44] They were doubtless placed decoratively among the feathers, to add both colour and fragrance.[45] The base of the shade, as has been said, was usually semicircular, but elaborate variations are known. The empty stock of a shade of Twenty-Second Dynasty date is surmounted by an image of Bes who bears the cartouche of one of the Takelots upon his head. The sides of Bes and of the cartouche are perforated with holes for the insertion of the ostrich feathers.[46]

We have called the *bht* a sunshade, and such it undoubtedly was; but there is evidence that it was also used as a fan. One of the handles from Tutankhamun's tomb is bent at right angles, a fact which suggests that a greater movement of air was desired than could normally be produced by rotating a straight handle.[47] Moreover, a scene from Amarna in which several sunshades appear supports the view that the *bht* doubled as a fan. The scene depicts Akhenaten and family taking a stroll in the sunshine. Although four persons close to the royal family are holding aloft large *bht*-shades, these are in no way shielding them from the sunlight, which is shown streaming down upon them from the Aten.[48] It might be argued that the priority given to the motif of the many-armed sun, shedding its protection and life upon the royal couple, prevented the artist from showing the sunshades fulfilling their proper function. But, on the other hand, when one recalls the emphasis on truth and "realism" in Amarna art, one wonders why a sunshade which did not provide shade from the sun would be shown at all. It is more likely that the *bht* in this scene did have a function, namely that of a fan. Another scene is even less ambiguous. From the Theban tomb of Tjay (reign of Merneptah) comes the scene of a scriptorium, where the chief scribe is accompanied by a servant holding up a small *bht* behind the great man's head. That the *bht* is being used as a fan is proved, not only by a neighbouring inscription referring to the heat, but by the fact that the entire scene is indoors.[49]

Though the appearance of the word *bht* is confined to the New Kingdom and later, an object of the same shape and use was

44 W. Erichsen, *Papyrus Harris I* (Brussels, 1933), p. 24.

45 *Pace* J. H. Breasted, *Ancient Records of Egypt* (5 vols.; Chicago, 1906), IV, §244, n. *b*.

46 Z. Saad, *ASAE* 42 (1942), pp. 147ff., pl. 13.

47 Carter, *The Tomb of Tut-ankh-amen*, III, p. 68.

48 Tomb of Parennefer: Davies, *El-Amarna*, VI, pl. 3; similarly III, pl. 13.

49 L. Borchardt, *ZÄS* 44 (1907), p. 59, Abb. 1; for similar employment of the *bht* as a fan, cf. Smith, *Art and Architecture*, pl. 170b; N. de G. Davies, *The Town House in Ancient Egypt* (Met. Mus. Stud. 1, 2; New York, 1929), fig. Ia, b.

known as early as Protodynastic times. On the Narmer mace-head from Hierakonpolis[50] two servants are depicted beneath the dais holding up long-handled flabella, the tops of which are semicircular. Though no internal detail is shown which might indicate of what material the objects were made, a slightly earlier representation on the mace-head of king "Scorpion"[51] shows two similar sunshades decorated with radiating columns of hatching. This is precisely the technique which in contemporary art is used to indicate the plumage of birds.[52] We are therefore justified in assuming that already at the dawn of Egyptian history feathers (probably of the ostrich) were used in the making of sunshade-fans. Objects of the same shape appear in the hands of symbols arranged behind the striding figure of Djoser in the reliefs of the Step-Pyramid complex.[53] They are seen again in the *sd*-festival reliefs from the Sun-temple of Neuserre. Here they are carried on the shoulder by courtiers, singly or in pairs, who follow the king's palanquin.[54] There is another fragmentary example from Montuhotpe II's temple at Deir el-Bahri, which gives the detail of the white and brown feathers.[55]

Probably at a very early time the two flabella which accompanied the king were personified in the god *Ḥp.wy*. The name may perhaps mean merely "the two flabella," from an unattested word *ḥp*.[56] As early as Pepy II this god appears together with two others who are likewise personifications of objects closely associated with the royal person.[57] The first is the king's beard. The second (*ḥq.s*) was thought by Sethe to be a designation of the breast ornament *qní*.[58] Both *Ḥp.wy* and *Ḥq.s* are later intimately connected with the delta, but it does not seem likely that this connection is original.[59]

We are right in terming the *ḥp* (if there was such a word) a

50 Quibell, *Hieraconpolis*, I, pl. 26 (B).

51 *Ibid.*, pl. 25.

52 *Ibid.*, pl. 6:6 (16:4).

53 E. Drioton and J.-P. Lauer, *Sakkarah, les monuments de Djoser* (Cairo, 1939), pls. 26, 27; cf. also G. Jéquier, *CdE* 27 (1939), p. 31.

54 Von Bissing and Kees, *Re-Heiligtum*, pl. 19, 17.

55 E. Naville, *The Eleventh Dynasty Temple at Deir el-Bahari* (3 vols.; London, 1907–13), pl. 20.

56 Kees (*ZÄS* 77 [1941], 26) connects it with *ḥp.ty*, "both ends (of the world)," which, however, appears to be attested from Greek times only: *Wörterbuch*, III, 69:11f.

57 Jéquier, *Monument funéraire*, II, pl. 60.

58 K. Sethe, *Übersetzung und Kommentar zu den altägyptischen Pyramidentexten* (4 vols.; Glückstadt, 1935–39), II, 244; or *ỉ3q.s*, see *Wörterbuch*, I, 33, and G. Thausing, *WZKM* 39 (1932), p. 292.

59 Naville, *Festival Hall*, p. 20; Gardiner, *JEA* 30 (1944), pp. 29f. (especially nn. 29, 30); B. Grdseloff, *BIFAO* 45 (1945), pp. 180f.; Kees, *ZÄS* 77, 26 n. 6.

sunshade and not a fan. Its use as a hieroglyphic determinative in the word *šw*, "shade, shadow," makes its basic function apparent.[60] As in the case of the *bht*, however, it may also have been employed as a fan.

The object carried by the courtier in the ROM relief is different from the semicircular sunshade discussed above. The earliest occurrence of such an object known to the author is on the relief from the Step-Pyramid showing Djoser engaged in the ceremonial dance.[61] Behind the king appear an ankh and a sceptre, the former bearing the object which we are now investigating and the latter a sunshade identical in shape with those of "Scorpion" and Narmer, though lacking the long handle. The ankh's burden, in contrast to the sunshade, has a head whose width is considerably less than its (vertical) length. Moreover, its lower edge forms a V-shaped cleft of about 90°, while the sunshade has a lower edge which is virtually straight.[62] The fact that the two objects are distinguished here, and are never confused in later Old Kingdom reliefs and paintings, implies that there is a basic difference between them, in construction certainly, and perhaps also in function. The same V-shaped cleft is usually present in later examples, but occasionally it is absent.[63] That this is only a variation of the type, however, is proved by both manner of carrying and by context.

The lotiform shape of the object is quite clear,[64] but it is difficult to decide whether the shape was suggested by that of a lotus leaf, or whether lotus leaves were used in its construction.[65] We do know that leaves of various plants and trees were used as fans. In scenes from New Kingdom tombs we see servants with large palm leaves in their hands, fanning jars of beer.[66] New Kingdom papyri make mention of packs of palm leaves, doubtless destined to be used as fans.[67] The leaf of the Dôm palm, especially, has been considered to be the object whose composition we are seeking.[68] Whether the

60 *Wörterbuch*, IV, 432.

61 Above, n. 53.

62 Because of the weight of the feathers, both ends are depicted as sagging slightly, as in the earlier examples of "Scorpion" and Narmer.

63 E.g. Z. Saad, *ASAE* 40 (1940), pl. 79; 42 (1942), pls. 14, 15.

64 G. Jéquier, *Frises d'objets des sarcophages du moyen empire* (*MIFAO* 47 [1921]), p. 254.

65 See L. Keimer, *ASAE* 28 (1928), pp. 38f.; *idem, REA* 2 (1930), p. 233, figs. 32–3; *idem, ASAE* 48 (1948), pp. 98f., figs. 10–13.

66 J. J. Tylor and F. Ll. Griffith, *The Tomb of Paheri at El Kab* (London, 1894), pl. 3 (second register, right); Davies, *The Tomb of Menkheperrasonb*, pl. 27.

67 For discussion and references, see R. A. Caminos, *Late Egyptian Miscellanies* (London, 1954), pp. 442f.

68 V. Loret, *Sphinx* 6 (1902), p. 110.

shape be that of a lotus or Dôm palm leaf, we may be sure that the material from which the better ones were made was something less perishable than plant fibre.

The lotiform flabellum was certainly used as a fan. This is proved by the fact that it appears as determinative in the word *nft*, "fan," a word derived from *nfw*, "wind."[69] One passage, in fact from the tomb of Fetekta at Saqqara,[70] not only writes the word with this determinative, but also shows the object itself in the form of a lotus-leaf-shaped fan with short handle. The inscription above the man holding it (who is offering it to a dealer for sale) records his words : "look at this fan which fans me!"[71] Further proof that this kind of flabellum was used as a fan and not as a sunshade is contained in a scene which occurs in the tombs of Parennefer and Tutu at Amarna.[72] In a store-room of the palace between two tall columns stand three rows of tressels holding jars of beer or the like. To one side stands a servant, vigorously fanning them with a fan in the shape of a lotus leaf. In an adjacent room another servant, armed with an identical object, is similarly employed. The object of the operation was undoubtedly to keep the liquid cool and to drive off the flies.[73]

During the Fourth and Fifth Dynasties the lotiform fan becomes relatively common,[74] and is found in both royal and private reliefs. Two forms can be distinguished on the basis of length of handle. The long-handled variety, which is what our courtier carries, was widely favoured by the king during the Old Kingdom,[75] probably simply because when he was elevated in a palanquin above the heads of his entourage no short-handled fan could reach him. The king

69 *Wörterbuch*, II, 250; the hide (F 27) is also used to determine this word, but only in Middle Egyptian.

70 Lepsius, *Denkmaeler*, II, 96; Porter and Moss, *Topographical Bibliography*, III, pp. 97f.

71 Loret, *Sphinx* 6 (1902), p. 111, who also cities a passage in A. Erman, *Zaubersprüche für Mutter und Kind* (Berlin, 1901), p. 38. I take *nfit* in the present inscription to be a perfective active participle, fem. sing., from *nfi* (*Wörterbuch*, II, 250:11); cf. E. Edel, *Altägyptische Grammatik* (Rome, 1955), § 628.

72 Davies, *El-Amarna*, VI, pl. 4, 19.

73 For a similar scene, carved on a block from the sanctuary of the royal estate at Amarna, see Pendlebury, *The City of Akhenaten*, III, pl. 47:4. For the short-handled *bht* similarly used, see T. Säve-söderbergh, *Four Eighteenth Dynaisty Tombs* (*Private Tombs at Thebes*, I; Oxford, 1957), p. 22.

74 E. Drioton, *ASAE* 41 (1941), p. 121.

75 Examples: Von Bissing and Kees, *Re-Heiligtum*, pls. 16:39, 18:44c; Saad, *ASAE* 40 (1940), pp. 683f., pl. 79; ; *ibid.*, 42 (1942), pls. 14–15; Sir W. M. F. Petrie, *The Palaces of Apries* (*Memphis II*), pl. 3 (Saite, but copied from an Old or Middle Kingdom original); Borchardt, *Ne-user-re'*, p. 85, Abb. 62c.

also made use of the latter,[76] and these are shown, especially at *sd*-festivals,[77] carried by a member of his personal staff along with a fly whisk. Private individuals of the Old Kingdom appropriated both types of fan. The long-handled fan is carried by a household servant behind the tomb owner, as in the royal reliefs;[78] frequently it is a woman who shoulders it, but apparently only when the scene shows the mistress of the house.[79] In nearly every case the posture of the bearer and the angle at which the fan lies on the shoulder are the same as in the ROM relief.[80] The short-handled fan is more common in private tombs. It is often carried by an unidentified servant in a line of servants who bear articles of their master's personal use.[81] The latter include garments, satchels, writing-desks, papyrus cases and the like, all frequently in charge of the "master of clothes,"[82] a servant whose task seems to have been to supervise the morning toilet.[83] The servants who carry the objects are shown in close attendance upon their master, waiting to refresh him, change his clothing perhaps, or provide him with the means to jot down a memorandum. As the king had required a sunshade-fan when he went abroad in his palanquin, so did the noble. Most frequently shade and air-flow were provided by a piece of fabric stretched on a square or rectangular (wooden?) frame, mounted on a long handle.[84] This, when elevated above the palanquin, would give shade, and a strip of cloth hanging at the back could be made to

76 Jéquier, *Monument funéraire*, II, pl. 16; *idem*, *La pyramide d'Aba* (Cairo, 1935), p. 24, fig. 7.

77 Von Bissing and Kees, *Re-Heiligtum*, pls. 9:20, 11:27, 13:33a, 19:44a, 20:47, 22:52.

78 Wreszinski, *Atlas*, III, Taf. 11, 408; J. Leibovitch, *ASAE* 39 (1939), p. 151, fig. 6; F. Ll. Griffith, *apud* Davies, *The Mastaba of Ptahhetep and Akhethetep*, II, pl. 8.

79 See previous note; also Saad, *ASAE* 40 (1940), pl. 79.

80 Cf., however, Wreszinski, *Atlas*, III, Taf. 11.

81 Lepsius, *Denkmaeler*, II, pls. 105a, 19, 30, 32 (more ovoid, but probably derived from the fan shaped like a lotus leaf), 87; H. Schaefer and W. Andrae, *Die Kunst des alten Orient* (3rd ed.; Berlin, 1942), p. 220; Reisner, *A History of the Giza Necropolis*, I (Cambridge, Mass., 1942), fig. 263; H. Junker, *Giza* (12 vols.; Vienna and Leipzig, 1929–55), VII, p. 73, Abb. 31 (ovoid, probably a fan); G. Steindorff, *Das Grab des Ti* (Leipzig, 1913), pls. 16, 17.

82 *Imy-r sšr* (*Wörterbuch*, IV, 296:4–6); cf., for example, Lepsius, *Denkmaeler*, II, pls. 37, 87, 104.

83 On the title, see Sir A. H. Gardiner, *BIFAO* 30 (1931), p. 173; W. Helck, *Untersuchungen zu den Beamtentiteln des ägyptischen alten Reiches* (Ägyptologische Forschungen, 18; Glückstadt, 1954), p. 66.

84 N. de G. Davies, *The Rock Tombs of Deir el-Gebrawi* (2 vols.; London, 1902), I, pl. 8; P. E. Newberry, *Beni Hasan* (2 parts; London, 1893), II, pl. 16; Junker, *Giza*, V, p. 85, Abb. 20; Lepsius, *Denkmaeler*, II, pls. 9, 78b; Wreszinski, *Atlas*, III, pl. 405.

flap to create a movement of air, and to drive the flies away. But upon occasion the short-handled, lotiform fan was substituted for this monstrous rectangular object. In an early Fourth Dynasty tomb from Giza[85] an empty palanquin is shown upon the shoulders of the servants, attended by the "eldest of the House, Meny." Upon the seat rests a short-handled fan, awaiting the personal use of the noble.[86]

As a functional object[87] the lotiform fan is not often depicted after the close of the Old Kingdom. A very few reliefs and paintings, however, show that it had not passed entirely out of use. At Deir el-Bahri a long-handled example is shown, resting across Hatshepsut's vacant throne on board ship.[88] An example of the short-handled variety comes from the tomb of Kenamun.[89] In a tomb of the time of Thutmose IV the owner is shown receiving a reward from the king. The owner's figure is now lost, but behind him and still preserved is the unmistakable outline of a lotiform fan hovering above his head.[90] Reminiscent of the fans of Old Kingdom royal reliefs are those shown on the large Saite relief which Petrie found at Memphis;[91] but these scenes are surely only copies of Old Kingdom originals. Though the object is not represented, the word denoting the sunshade-fan of Zakar-Baal of Byblos in the story of Wenamun[92] is provided with a lotus leaf as determinative. Whether this is an indication of the actual form of the fan, or merely recalls an ancestral, archaic type no longer used, is difficult to say; but the former may well be the case. Since Byblos had long had contacts

85 Junker, *Giza*, II, p. 185, Abb. 31.

86 A similar scene is found at Deir el-Bahri (E. Naville, *The Temple of Deir el-Bahari* [6 vols.; London, 1895–1908], VI, pl. 154). A throne reserved for Hatshepsut upon a royal barge supports, not the queen's figure, but a long-handled fan in the shape of a lotus leaf which rests upon it. For a *bht*-fan, apparently in the same position, see J. Lipinska, *ASAE* 59 (1966), pl. 16. During the *sd*-festival there was apparently a minor rite in which the two fans were placed across the king's throne, immediately after he had vacated it; cf. Naville, *The Festival Hall of Osorkon II*, pl. 21. The inscription above the two fan-bearers mounting the dais reads "going forth, placing (?) the fans upon the throne"; see E. Uphill, *JNES* 24 (1965), p. 380.

87 For the use of the flabellum in the shape of a lotus leaf in the New Kingdom as a symbol of protection behind the king, see Kees, *Opfertanz*, pp. 120ff.

88 Above, n. 86.

89 N. de G. Davies, *The Tomb of Kenamun at Thebes* (The Metropolitan Museum of Art Egyptian Expedition, 5; New York, 1930), pl. 5a.

90 N. de G. Davies, *The Tombs of Two Officials of Thutmosis the Fourth* (EES Theban Tomb Series, 3; London, 1923), pl. 12.

91 Above, n. 75.

92 Wenamun, 2, 45. The word is *srpt*, Coptic *сарпот*; see *Wörterbuch*, IV, 195:4; also Sir A. H. Gardiner, *Late Egyptian Stories* (Brussels, 1932), p. 71a (note).

with Egypt, Zakar-Baal's fan probably derives from the Egyptian type, if it is not actually of Egyptian manufacture.

On the identity of the fan-bearer in the relief under discussion it is impossible to say much. The names of fan-bearers are only rarely given in private reliefs,[93] and never in royal. The most we could hope for would be a title, but, as pointed out above, the partially preserved hieroglyphs probably refer to the falcon and the king, not to the fan-bearers. We are obliged, then, to argue solely from analogy.

Two grades of royal servant are shown carrying fans in the *sd*-festival reliefs of the Old Kingdom. One is the *ẖry-nw.s*, the other the *ỉmy-ḫnt*.[94] The former occurs by himself in a file of servants, sometimes at the head, always in the immediate vicinity of the king.[95] His task was to carry the small, portable objects, such as sceptre, crook, flail, fan, etc., which the king would need in the course of the ritual; and to this end he had always to stand close to the king ready to hand over a particular item of paraphernalia when it was needed. His title, "bearer of the *nw.s*," signifies his most important (or his original ?) function, but one which he seems never to be shown performing. *Nw.s* is a word denoting a particular and rare type of crown, possibly of Lower Egyptian origin. It probably once fell to the *ẖry-nw.s* to look after this crown, and hold it at the ceremony of the coronation, a charge later broadened to include sceptres, sandals, fans, etc. used by the king.[96] The fan carried by this servant in Old Kingdom reliefs is usually short-handled,[97] and this together with the fact that he does have a colleague seems to exclude him from candidacy in the present case. The other type of courtier who is shown carrying a fan is the *ỉmy-ḫnt*, lit. "he who is in front/in the 'presence' (of the king ?)."[98] The tasks which devolved upon this type of *valet de chambre* concerned mainly the robing and adorning of the king,[99] carrying his palanquin on ex-

93 One example in Lepsius, *Denkmaeler*, II, pl. 30.

94 In the Late Period the *śmr* also may carry a fan; cf. Naville, *The Festival Hall of Osorkon II*, pl. 2.

95 Von Bissing and Kees, *Re Heiligtum*, pls. 13:33b, 14:35, 19:44a, 20:47. Cf. also, from a later period, A. Fakhry, *ASAE* 42 (1942), p. 493; Naville, *The Festival Hall of Osorkon II*, pls. 1, 19, 21, 23, 24 (kneeling on a dais).

96 On the *ẖry-nw.s* see Jéquier, *MIFAO* 47, p. 6; H. Junker, *ASAE* 49 (1949), pp. 211f.; R. Weill, *RdE* 7 (1950), pp. 185f.; Helck, *Beamtentiteln*, p. 24.

97 Sometimes a long-handled fan in the Late Period; see Naville, *The Festival Hall of Osorkon II*, pls. 19, 23.

98 Or "he who is in the forehall" ? Cf. H. Kees, *Aegypten* (*Kulturgeschichte des Alten Orients*, I; Munich, 1933), p. 180; Helck, *Beamtentiteln*, p. 29.

99 Sir A. H. Gardiner, *JEA* 39 (1953), pp. 26f.

cursions abroad,[100] and shading him.[101] In performing this last occupation these courtiers are depicted in exactly the same position and stance as the fan-bearer in the ROM relief. There can be little doubt, then, although he is not so designated in the fragment preserved, that this courtier is an *ỉmy-ḫnt*.[102]

As for the date of the relief, it seems safe to say that it cannot be earlier than Sneferu or later than the middle of the Fifth Dynasty. But between these two extremes there is a wide range and the paucity of comparative material precludes any attempt at closer dating. If the delicate low relief suggests the Fourth Dynasty, the content of the scene calls to mind the Fifth; I can see no way at present of choosing between them.

100 Von Bissing and Kees, *Re-Heiligtum*, pls. 18:44a, c, 19:45a, b, 20:46.

101 *Ibid.*, pl. 19:45, a, b.

102 For the religious functions which increasingly gave the *ỉmy-ḫnt* the appearance of a priest, see L. Habachi, *ASAE* 47 (1947), pp. 261f.; K. Sethe, *apud* Borchardt, *Saȝhure'*, II, 96; H. Gauthier, *Le Personel du dieu Min* (Cairo, 1931), pp. 62f.; W. C. Hayes, *JNES* 10 (1951), p. 101, n. 224.

The Passive *Qal* Theme in Hebrew

RONALD J. WILLIAMS

The presence of a passive of the *Qal* theme in biblical Hebrew was recognized by Böttcher a century ago,[1] subsequently discussed by Barth,[2] referred to by Bergsträsser in his revision of the monumental grammar of Gesenius,[3] and treated at some length by Bauer and Leander.[4] However, despite the apparent acceptance of their findings, it is more than a little puzzling to note the reluctance with which later scholars have treated the passive *Qal*. The standard Hebrew lexicon in English[5] accepts the form without question only in the case of the root ŠGL, and merely mentions its possibility for the roots HRY, NTN, NTṢ, SYK, 'ZB, ŠDD, and ŠYT. The most recent revision of Davidson's Hebrew grammar refers only to forms of the roots LQḤ and NTN as "probably ... the old passive Qal."[6] This is the more surprising in view of the fact that more than fifty Hebrew roots preserve forms which may properly be classed as passive *Qal*. Perhaps it will not be amiss, then, for us to assemble the evidence with respect to this form.

It is well known that literary Arabic alone of the Semitic languages has retained the passive of the *Qal* theme as a living form, with the perfect aspect assuming the pattern /qutila/, "he was

1 F. Böttcher, *Ausführliches Lehrbuch der hebräischen Sprache* (Leipzig, 1868), vol. II, §§ 904–6, 1022.

2 J. Barth, "Das passive Qal und seine Participien," *Jubelschrift zum siebzigsten Geburtstag des Dr. Israel Hildesheimer* (Berlin, 1890), pp. 145ff.

3 F. H. W. Gesenius, *Hebräische Grammatik*, 29th ed. rev. by G. Bergsträsser (Leipzig, 1918–29), vol. II, § 15.

4 H. Bauer and P. Leander, *Historische Grammatik der hebräischen Sprache* (Halle, 1922), § 38 l′–r′.

5 F. Brown, S. R. Driver, and C. A. Briggs, *A Hebrew and English Lexicon of the Old Testament* (Oxford, 1906).

6 A. B. Davidson, *An Introductory Hebrew Grammar*, 25th ed. rev. by J. Mauchline (Edinburgh, 1962), p.159.

killed," complemented by the imperfect /yuqtalu/. In Aramaic the perfect aspect alone remains, e.g. /yᵊhīḇ/, "it was given." This displays a secondary lengthening of the vowel on the analogy of the passive participle (originally an adjectival pattern). For other evidence we must turn to the remains of early Northwest Semitic.

As Böhl[7] and Ebeling[8] demonstrated independently, the cuneiform tablets from the fourteenth century B.C. Egyptian royal archives at Tell el-Amarna are especially instructive for this purpose.[9] Many of these letters from the rulers of the city states in Palestine and Syria to their Egyptian suzerain contain glosses and grammatical forms which betray the native Canaanite speech of their writers. Happily the syllabic nature of the cuneiform script, unlike most Semitic writing systems, provides us with evidence for the vocalization. In the missives from Rib-Addi of Byblos we encounter verbal forms with passive meaning such as the following: *yú-ul-qí*, "it will be taken" (EA 105/82); *tu-ul-qú*, "it (f.) will be taken" (EA 132/15); *tu-ṣa-bat*, "it (f.) will be captured" (EA 85/46); *yú-da-na*, "it is to be given" (EA 86/32, 47); *tu-da-nu-na*, "they (f.) were given" (EA 83/23); *tu-uš-mu-na*, "they (f.) were heard" (EA 89/37, 122/55). Other letters from Byblos and from Milkili of Gezer contain the form *yú-pa-šu*, "it will be done" (EA 114/42, 138/74 f., 271/21, 272/21), written *yú-up-pa-šu* in a document from Acco (EA 232/20).

We turn next to the extensive body of Ugaritic texts from the fifteenth and fourteenth centuries B.C.[10] In these North Syrian mythological poems and other documents we are faced with the ambiguity of an unvocalized script. Fortunately the use of three different signs to represent the glottal stop, intended to indicate the accompanying vowel, makes it possible for us to determine the vocalization of passive forms of verbs which have this phoneme as the first or second radical. Thus we find the form *yủḫd*, "it was kindled" (51.iv.16), to be read /yu'ḫad/,[11] contrasting with the active form *yiḫd*, "he seized" (49.v.1), probably to be vocalized

7 F. M. T. Böhl, "Die Sprache der Amarnabriefe," *LSS* v, 2 (1909), § 30.

8 E. Ebeling, "Das Verbum der El-Amarna Briefe," *BA* 8/2 (1910), § 11.

9 J. A. Knudtzon, *Die El-Amarna Tafeln* (*VAB*, vol. II; Leipzig, 1907–15).

10 Cited in accordance with C. H. Gordon, *Ugaritic Textbook* (*Analecta Orientalia*, 38; Rome, 1965).

11 We must record the baffling forms *tủḫd* (137/40), for which the context demands the meaning "let her take," *yủhb*, "he loved (67. v. 18), and *yủkl*, "he will have the usufruct of" (1081/16); cf. the normal form *tikl* (51.vi.24, 29). Gordon compares the anomalous Hebrew *Qal* forms /yūḵal/ and /nɔʿɔḇᵊḏēm/ (Deut. 13:3); cf. also /tɔʿɔḇᵊḏēm/ (Exod. 20:5, 23:24; Deut. 5:9).

/ye'ḫud/.[12] A second verb occurs in the form *tlảkn* (51.v.104), indicating the pronunciation /tul'akūna/, which is to be rendered "they were sent." In the preceding line of the same text *yảkl* is commonly agreed to be a metathesis for *ylảk*, i.e. /yul'ak/, "he was sent."

The passive is sometimes expressed in Ugaritic by the *Niph'al* theme. Where the N-prefix has been assimilated to a following consonant, it is impossible to distinguish these forms from those of the passive *Qal*. However, in the case of roots having N as the first radical, the theme with prefixed N is excluded. Such are *td*, "it (f.) was extinguished" (51.vi.32, from NDY); *tdr*, "it (f.) was vowed" (128.iii.23, from NDR); *ysk*, "it will be poured out" (2 Aq vi.36, from NSK); *tṣb*, "it (f.) is set" (2 Aq vi. 13, from NṢB).[13] Other clear cases of the passive *Qal* are found with roots beginning with W/Y. Such are *ytn*, "let it be given" (52/3, from YTN), probably to be read /yūtan/ and *ybl*, "it is brought" (52/52, 59, from YBL), most likely pronounced /yūbal/.

All these examples have been of the preformative conjugation. The afformative conjugation is rare with fientive verbs, but instances of the passive *Qal* may be cited. Such are *yld*, "he was born" (2 Aq ii.14; this might also be interpreted as a preformative conjugation); *hry*, "he was conceived" (132/5); *ġly*, "it was lowered" (1 Aq 160); and *št*, "they have been put" (2106/3, from ŠYT), distinguished in meaning but not in written form from *št*, "he placed" (51.v.107).[14]

The limitations imposed by a consonantal script make the identification of passive *Qal* forms in Phoenician well-nigh impossible. The only likely example is found in two Punic inscriptions of the third or early second century B.C., viz. *št*, "it was put" (*KAI* 69/17 f., 20, 74/11).

The evidence thus marshalled is clearly in favour of the existence of a passive of the *Qal* theme in the West Semitic languages exhibiting the pattern *CuCiCa/yuCCaCu* which contrasts with the active pattern *CaCaCa/yaCCuCu*. The assumption that such a passive form was also a feature of Hebrew is natural enough. However, just as in Ugaritic and Phoenician, the *Niph'al* theme, origi-

12 The unique *yảḫd* (93/11) might be an instance of the disputed present-future /ya'aḫadu/ postulated by Goetze and Harris.

13 Driver, however, derives this from a root ṢBW, and translates "she coveted."

14 The twice-repeated expression *ủḫd b'lm* (1001/6, 14) might preserve another instance of the afformative conjugation of the passive *Qal*. If so, the vowel accompanying the initial consonant would be a welcome confirmation of the vocalization. However, the context is damaged and too obscure for certainty.

nally with reflexive or middle and reciprocal force, came to be used also to express the passive idea. Consequently, the passive *Qal* became increasingly less common, until by the time of biblical Hebrew it was obsolescent. Many traces still survived in the masoretic text, which may now be listed :

(1) 'KL, "eat": Perf. /'ukkᵊlū/ (Neh. 2:3, 13; Nah. 1:10); Imperf. /tᵊ'ukkᵊlū/ (Isa. 1:20); Partic. /'ukkɔ̄l/ (Exod. 3:2).
(2) 'SR, "bind": Perf. /'ussᵊrū/ (Isa. 22:3, *bis*).
(3) 'RR, "curse": Imperf. /yū'ɔ̄r/ (pausal, Num. 22:6).
(4) BZZ, "plunder": Perf. /buzzɔ̄zū/ (pausal, Jer. 50:37).
(5) DWŠ, "thresh": Imperf. /yūḏaš/ (Isa. 28:27).
(6) DḤW, "thrust down": Perf. /dōḥū/ (Ps. 36:13).
(7) HGW, "utter": Absol. Inf. /hōḡō/ (Isa. 59:13).
(8) HGY/W, "remove": Perf. /hōḡɔ̄/ (II Sam. 20:13).[15]
(9) HRG, "kill": Perf. /hōrɔ̄ḡ/ (pausal, Isa. 27:7), /hōraḡnū/ (Ps. 44:23).
(10) HRY, "conceive": Perf. /hōrɔ̄/ (Job 3:3); Absol. Inf. /hōrō/ (Isa. 59:13).
(11) ZWR, "squeeze": Perf. /zōrū/ (Isa. 1:6).
(12) ZNY, "fornicate": Perf. /zunnɔ̄/ (Ezek. 16:34).
(13) ZRW, "winnow": Partic. /zōrɛ̄/ (Isa. 30:24).
(14) ZR', "sow": Perf. /zōrɔ̄'ū/ (pausal, Isa. 40:24).
(15) ZRQ, "sprinkle": Perf. /zōraq/ (Num. 19:13, 20).
(16) ḤWL, "give birth": Imperf. /yūḥal/ (Isa. 66:8).
(17) ḤNN, "show favour": Imperf. /yūḥan/ (Isa. 26:10; Prov. 21:10).
(18) ḤṢB, "hew": Perf. /ḥuṣṣaḇtɛm/ (Isa. 51:1).
(19) ḤQQ, "incise": Imperf. /yūḥɔ̄qū/ (pausal, Job 19:23); Partic./ mᵊḥuqqɔ̄q/ (Prov. 31:5).
(20) ṬRP, "tear": Perf. /ṭōrap̄/ (Gen. 37:33, 44:28).
(21) YLD, "give birth": Perf. /yullaḏ/ (Gen. 4:26; Judg. 18:29, etc.), /yullᵊḏū /(Gen. 6:1, 36:5, etc.); Partic. /yullɔ̄d/ (Judg. 13:8).
(22) YṢR, "form": Perf. /yuṣṣɔ̄rū/ (pausal, Ps. 139:16); Imperf. /yūṣar/ (Isa. 54:17).
(23) YQŠ, "snare": Partic. /yūqɔ̄šīm/ (Eccles. 9:12).
(24) YŠB, "inhabit": Imperf. /tūšɔ̄ḇ/ (pausal, Isa. 44:26).
(25) KRT, "cut": Perf. /kɔrraṯ/ (with *daghesh* abnormally in the R, Ezek. 16:4), /kōrɔ̄ṯɔ̄/ (pausal, Judg. 6:28).
(26) LQḤ, "take": Perf. /luqqaḥ/ (Gen. 3:23; Judg. 17:2, etc.), /luqqᵊḥū/ (Jer. 48:46); Imperf. /yuqqaḥ/ (Gen. 18:4; Job 28:2, etc.), /tuqqaḥ/ (Gen. 12:15); Partic. /luqqɔ̄ḥ/ (II Kings 2:10).
(27) MRṬ, "polish": Perf. /mōrɔ̄ṭṭɔ̄/ (pausal, with an unexpected doubling of the Ṭ in both cases, Ezek. 21:15f.); Partic. /mōrɔ̄ṭ/ (Isa. 18:2, 7), /mᵊmōrɔ̄ṭ/ (I Kings 7:45).

15 Regarded as a *Hiph'il* perfect from an assumed root YGW by Brown, Driver, and Briggs, *Hebrew Lexicon.*

(28) MRQ, "scour": Perf. /mōraq/ (Lev. 6:21).
(29) NṬŠ, "forsake": Perf. /nuṭṭōš/ (pausal, Isa. 32:14).
(30) NPḤ, "blow on": Perf. /nuppōḥ/ (pausal, Job 20:26), /nōp̄aḥ/ (Num. 21:30).
(31) NQM, "avenge": Imperf. /yuqqam/ (Gen. 4:15, 24; Exod. 21:21).
(32) NTN, "give": Imperf. /yuttan/ (1 Kings 2:21; Lev. 11:38, etc.).
(33) NTṢ, "break": Imperf. /yuttōṣ/ (pausal, Lev. 11:35).
(34) NTŠ, "pluck": Imperf. /tuttaš/ (Ezek. 19:12).
(35) SWK, "pour, anoint": Imperf. /yūsōḵ/ (pausal, Exod. 30:32, Sam. Pent.; MT has /yīsōḵ/!).
(36) ʻBD, "work": Perf. /ʻubbaḏ/ (Deut. 21:3; Isa. 14:3.
(37) ʻZB, "forsake": Perf. /ʻuzzōḇ/ (pausal, Isa. 32:14), /ʻuzzᵊḇō/ (Jer. 49:25).
(38) ʻMM, "darken": Imperf. /yūʻam/ (Lam. 4:1).
(39) ʻŚW/Y, "make": Perf. /ʻuśśēṯī/ (Ps. 139:15).
(40) QBR, "bury": Perf. /qubbar/ (Gen. 25:10).
(41) QR', "call": Perf. /qōrō/ (Isa. 48:8; Ezek. 10:13, etc.); Partic. /mᵊqōrō'ī (Isa. 48:12).
(42) QRṢ, "break off": Perf. /qōraṣtī/ (Job 33:6).
(43) R'Y, "see": Perf. /ru'ū/ (Job 33:21).
(44) Rʻ ʻ, "break": Partic. /rōʻō/ (Prov. 25:19).
(45) ŚYM, "put": Imperf. /yūśam/ (Gen. 24:33, *Qᵊrē*; Gen. 50:26, Sam. Pent.; MT has /yīśɛm/!).
(46) ŚRP, "burn": Perf. /śōrōp̄/ (pausal, Lev. 10:16).
(47) ŠGL, "lie with": Perf. /šuggalt/ (Jer. 3:2; *Qᵊrē* /šukkaḇt/).
(48) ŠDD, "destroy": Perf. /šuddaḏ/ (Isa. 15:1; Jer. 49:10, etc.), /šuddᵊḏō/ (Jer. 4:20; Zech. 11:3), /šuddᵊḏū/ (Jer. 4:20; Zech. 11:3); Imperf. /yuššaḏ/ (Hos. 10:14), /tūšaḏ/ (Isa. 33:1).[16]
(49) ŠṬP, "rinse": Perf. /šuṭṭap̄/ (Lev. 6:21).
(50) ŠYR, "sing": Imperf. /yūšar/ (Isa. 26:1).
(51) ŠYT, "place": Imperf. /yūšaṯ/ (Exod. 21:30).
(52) ŠPK, "pour": Perf. /šuppaḵ/ (Zeph. 1:17; Num. 35:33), /šuppᵊḵō/ (Ps. 73:2; *Qᵊrē* /šuppᵊḵū/).

The first fact that strikes our attention is that the verbs which have forms of the perfect aspect all exhibit a vocalization identical with the *Puʻal* theme. Occasionally this displays a *plene* writing with W for short /u/. The relevant examples are (12) /zunnō/, (21) /yullaḏ/ (Judg. 18:29; Job 5:7), as likewise in the imperfect (48) /yuššaḏ/ and /tuššaḏ/. In two cases the middle radical, although neither a laryngeal, pharyngeal, nor /r/, is not doubled, but the vowel /u/ is lengthened: (8) /hōḡɔ/ and (30) /nōp̄aḥ/.

16 So Kittel, *Biblia Hebraica*, 3rd ed. In some editions these forms are vocalized /yūšaḏ/ and /tuššaḏ/ respectively. It is apparent from the other geminating roots (3, 17, 19, 38) that the original forms were /yūšaḏ/ and /tūšaḏ/.

The second fact is that, with one exception, all imperfect forms are identical with those of the *Hoph'al* theme. The single anomaly is (1) /tᵊ'ukkᵊlū/, which has the form of a *Pu'al*, and may be a later, mistaken pronunciation. However, all other roots are initial W/Y, medial W/Y, initial N (L in the case of LQḤ), or geminating, and the initial consonant of 'KL may be responsible for the unusual vocalization (cf. the strange *Qal* form /tᵊ'ɔk̲lēhū/ in Job 20:26).

Six roots preserve participles which resemble those of the *Pu'al* without prefixed M (1, 13, 21, 26, 27, 44). A seventh, (23) /yūqɔ̄šīm/, is similar to a *Hoph'al* with initial Y in place of M. Contrasting with these are three exceptional forms identical with the *Pu'al*, viz. (19) /mᵊḥuqqɔ̄q/, (27) /mᵊmōrɔ̄ṭ/ (although the normal /mōrɔ̄ṭ/ occurs twice), and (41) /mᵊqōrɔ̄'ī/. The first might have acquired its prefix from an original enclitic M and the second by dittography, but the third is amenable to neither of these explanations. Perhaps the simplest solution is just to assume that scribes "corrected" the unusual forms to normal *Pu'al* participles. The lack of the prefix M is a characteristic of the *Qal* (and *Niph'al*) participle as distinct from those of the derived themes.[17]

The two forms identified as absolute infinitives (7, 10) resemble those of the *Pu'al* theme. The middle radical of the first example /hōḡō/ is not doubled, but the preceding vowel is lengthened as in the case of the perfect forms /hōḡɔ̄/ and /nōp̄aḥ/ discussed above.

It has been customary to regard most of the forms we have listed as either *Pu'al* or *Hoph'al*, but it would be strange indeed to find verbs exhibiting *Pu'al* perfects but *Hoph'al* imperfects, as the above evidence seems to indicate (22, 26, 48). Even more significant is the fact that twenty-nine of these verbs which have perfects resembling *Pu'al* forms (1, 2, 4, 6, 8, 9, 10, 11, 12, 14, 15, 18, 20, 22, 25, 26, 27, 28, 29, 30, 36, 37, 39, 41, 42, 43, 47, 49, 52) do not possess a *Pi'el* theme. The few exceptions are: (21) YLD, which in the *Pi'el* has a causative meaning "act as midwife"; (40) QBR, the *Pi'el* of which has a plurative sense, unsuitable here; (46) ŚRP, which has a single instance of a doubtful *Pi'el* participle (spelled with S for Ś! Amos 6:10); and (48) ŠDD, which exhibits *Pi'el* forms twice (Prov. 19:26, 24:15), but has a passive imperfect which cannot be *Pu'al*.

17 The form *Cɔ̄CūC* commonly regarded as the *Qal* passive participle is really an adjectival pattern pressed into service when the true participle was becoming obsolescent. Bergsträsser's claim (*Hebräische Grammatik*, vol. II, § 15) that the formation *CiC.ōC*, e.g. /'ērōm/, "naked," and the unusually vocalized /zērūᵃ'/, "sown," is a rare alternative of the form *Cɔ̄CūC* is surely mistaken. It rather represents the Proto-Semitic nominal formation *CaC.āC* from which were derived such forms as /gibbōr/ and /šikkōr/.

The form (20) /ṭōrap̄/ might properly be regarded as the passive of a plurative *Pi'el*, even though such does not occur, but the use of a *Qal* absolute infinitive for emphasis before both of the examples quoted speaks against it. On the other hand, the form /ḥuppɔ̄šɔ̄/ (Lev. 19:20), which has been cited as a passive *Qal*, is surely *Pu'al*, the passive of an unrecorded factitive *Pi'el* meaning "free" from a stative root ḤPŠ, "be free."

Sixteen verbs with imperfects which resemble *Hoph'al* forms (1, 3, 5, 17, 19, 22, 26, 31, 32, 33, 34, 35, 38, 48, 50, 51) lack the *Hiph'il* theme. The exceptions are: (16) ḤWL, the *Hiph'il* of which means "cause to be in anguish"; (24) YŠB, with a *Hiph'il* meaning "settle," and a corresponding *Hoph'al* with the sense "be made to dwell" (Isa. 5:8); and (45) ŚYM, which has doubtful *Hiph'il* forms in three passages (Ezek. 14:8, 21:21; Job 4:20).

When we examine the participles, six verbs (1, 19, 26, 27, 41, 44) have no *Pi'el*, and the seventh (23) lacks both *Pi'el* and *Hiph'il*. The two exceptions are (13) ZRW, which has both *Pi'el* and *Pu'al* in a plurative sense, with the normal participle /mᵊzōrɔ̄/ (Prov. 1:17), and (21) YLD, which, as noted above, has a *Pi'el* with a special meaning. The first mentioned form /zōrɔ̄/ might be construed as an active *Qal* participle but for the fact that the meaning required is passive. The two verbs which furnish us with examples of the absolute infinitive (7, 10) likewise have no recorded instances of the *Pi'el* theme.

The preponderance of perfect over imperfect forms (32 to 19) would appear to be significant. Eight of the roots lacking passive *Qal* imperfects have *Niph'al* imperfects which differ from the passive *Qal* only in vocalization. These are the following: (6) DḤW (Prov. 14:32; perhaps also the form /yiddaḥū/ in Jer. 23:12); (9) HRG (Lam. 2:20; Ezek. 26:6);[18] (18) ḤṢB (Job 19:24); (20) ṬRP (Exod. 22:12;[19] Jer. 5:6); (27) MRṬ (Lev. 13:40f.); (46) ŚRP (Josh. 7:15; Prov. 6:27); (47) ŠGL (Isa. 13:16; Zech. 14:2); (49) ŠṬP (Lev. 15:12; Dan. 11:22). Now, of those roots preserving *Qal* passive imperfect forms, all but 'KL are either geminating (3, 17, 19, 38, 48), with initial N (31, 32, 33, 34) or L (26), initial W/Y (22, 24), or medial W/Y (5, 16, 35, 45, 50, 51). Only in the case of 'KL or the initial W root YŠB could the consonantal skeletons of these forms be read as *Niph'al*. The conclusion is inescapable

18 The form /bēhɔ̄rēḡ/ (Ezek. 26:15), vocalized as a defectively written *Niph'al* construct infinitive, is generally regarded as a mispointed *Qal* infinitive, i.e. /bahᵃrōḡ/.

19 Note that here too the emphasizing absolute infinitive appears in the *Qal* theme.

that the marked lack of *Qal* passive imperfect forms in strong roots is the result of their being read as *Niph'al* forms.

We may summarize the history of the passive *Qal* in Hebrew in the following way. The original perfect /*kutiba/ became /*kutaba/ on the analogy of the perfects of all other passive themes. The normal phonetic development of Hebrew would eventually have produced a form /*kōṯaḇ/, but such an evolution was arrested when the form ceased to be a living one and was "fossilized" at some period before the lengthening of pretonic vowels. The original short /u/ was retained by the Masoretes, as was the short /a/ of the *waw*-consecutive, in the only possible way, viz. by doubling the following consonant to produce /*kuttaḇ/. This, of course, now meant that the form was indistinguishable from a *Pu'al*. The imperfect /*yuktabu/ by the same period had undergone the regular phonetic changes to become /*yuḵtaḇ/ or even /*yɔḵtaḇ/, which presents the same pattern as a *Hoph'al*. The participle, originally /*kutabu/, also acquired a doubled consonant like the perfect, and after the usual sound changes became /*kuttōḇ/.

With the extension of the range of meaning of the *Niph'al* theme to include that of a passive for the *Qal* in place of the true *Qal* passive, the latter rapidly decreased in frequency. Leaving out of account the roots YLD, LQḤ, and NTN, which are relatively common, we observe that almost exactly twice as many of the passive *Qal* forms occur in poetry as in prose. This is to be expected in view of the well-known propensity of poetry to preserve archaic forms. It would be natural for readers of the unvocalized Hebrew text to interpret passive forms as *Niph'al* wherever possible. This was ruled out, of course, in the case of the perfect aspect (except with initial N roots), the participle, and the infinitive. The consonantal framework of the *Qal* passive imperfect, however, was indistinguishable from that of the *Niph'al* with the exception of roots having initial N or medial W/Y, or those which were geminating, and many original *Qal* passives are probably now concealed as *Niph'al* imperfects.

Studies in the Palestinian Vocalization of Hebrew

E. J. REVELL

I THE VOWELS OF PALESTINIAN HEBREW AND THE HISTORY OF THE LANGUAGE*

Introduction

1 It is well known that three styles of 'pointing' were used to vocalize Hebrew in mediaeval times: the Palestinian, the Babylonian, and the Tiberian. The last named, used in a system which will here be called the 'ben Asher biblical'[1] (= bA), became the standard method of pointing Hebrew. It uses seven basic vowel signs, and one simple and three composite *shewa* signs. The Babylonian style of pointing (= Bab.) used only six basic vowel signs.[2] Not only the number of the signs, but also their use, makes it obvious that this pointing represents a pronunciation quite different from that represented by bA.[3] Bab. and bA are, therefore, said to represent different dialects of Hebrew.

* An earlier draught of this study was read before the Canadian Biblical Society, May 1965.

1 Neither of the common terms is satisfactory. 'Tiberian' indicates the style of pointing, the form and position of the signs. This style was used in a number of ways, of which bA was one. 'Masoretic' indicates only that a text was the subject of masoretic care, and can correctly be applied not only to bA texts, but also to Palestinian, Babylonian, and non-bA Tiberian traditions such as the so-called Ben Naftali.

2 Besides the major divisions of 'simple' and 'complex' pointing different 'systems' of using Babylonian points can be isolated (e.g. the 'Tiberianizing' ones which create new signs to correspond to bA *segol*, as in mss. 7a, b, c; 36, 38c, 40c, in Kahle, 1913).

3 For instance, the 'Babylonian *pataḥ*' (עַ) is usually said to correspond to bA *pataḥ* and *segol*. However, the Babylonian 'e' sign (as in *'t*, the 'sign of the definite

2 The Palestinian pointing system, like bA, uses seven vowel signs: ⟨u⟩, ⟨o⟩, ⟨a⟩, ⟨a′⟩, ⟨e⟩, ⟨e′⟩, and ⟨i⟩.[4] Of these, ⟨u⟩, ⟨o⟩, and ⟨i⟩ correspond almost exactly in use to bA *shureq/qibbuṣ*,[5] *ḥolem*, and *ḥireq*. In some mss., ⟨a⟩, ⟨a′⟩, ⟨e⟩, and ⟨e′⟩ are used almost exactly as bA uses *qameṣ*, *pataḥ*, *segol*, and *ṣere*. Other mss. use all four, or only three of these signs quite differently from the use of the bA signs. Such mss. use the two 'a' and the two 'e' signs with no very obvious discrimination, so that it appears to most students of these mss. that either 'a' sign can represent any 'a' vowel and either 'e' sign any 'e' vowel. In fact, in such mss., pairs of grammatically identical forms can usually be found in one of which ⟨a⟩, and in the other ⟨a′⟩, is used to represent the same vowel. The same is true for ⟨e⟩ and ⟨e′⟩. This fact, together with the existence of a further group of mss. which use only one 'a' and one 'e' sign, has led some scholars to conclude that Pal. represents a dialect which contained only one 'a' and one 'e' vowel.[6] The use of two 'a' and two 'e' signs is held to be due to the influence of bA. The opinion most generally accepted seems to be that Pal. developed from the use of one 'a' and one 'e' sign to the use of two of each, and from 'non-bA' to 'bA type' use of these signs.[7] Some scholars, however, argue that there is no real difference between the Palestinian dialect and that represented by bA. Those mss. which do not use the signs as does bA are held to be the work of ignorant *naqdanim*.[8]

3 This paper is an attempt to interpret the facts which came to light during the study and classification of the known Hebrew texts with Palestinian vocalization. A detailed study of the classification, together with some of the unpublished texts on which it is based, is

---

object') and the 'i' sign (as in the preposition *'l*) are also used where bA uses *segol*. Such usage is normally constant, and is not the result of vowel confusion. The area covered by *segol* in bA is, therefore, part of the area of use of three different signs in Bab. So also none of the other five Bab. vowel signs is used in exactly the same way as its 'corresponding' bA sign.

4 The signs are: ⟨u⟩ ¨ (∵), ⟨o⟩ ∴, ⟨a⟩ ˈ, ⟨a′⟩ ⁻, ⟨e⟩ ⋰, ⟨e′⟩ ⋱, ⟨i⟩ ⁚. The Tiberian names are not used for the obvious reason that such a practice would be confusing and tends to prejudice the evaluation of the signs.

5 *Shureq* and *qibbuṣ* are allographs of the Tiberian 'u' grapheme (see Schramm, 1964, p. 26). '*Shureq*' in this study is normally used to indicate this 'u' grapheme. One Palestinian ms. uses no ⟨u⟩ sign. See note 44.

6 Most recently, I think, Weinreich, 1964, p. 230.

7 This view has become standardized to the extent that it is given without supporting argument in Yeivin, 1963, pp. 123, 127.

8 See ben David, 1958, p. 483, who says of Palestinian Hebrew (top of col. b): "Its pronunciation was like true Tiberian, merely (written) in different signs." Usage divergent from bA is said to be due to ignorance (p. 484).

being published elsewhere.[9] The classification is, however, basic to the present study, and so is given in simplified form here. It is based on the use of the ‘a’ and ‘e’ signs in the Palestinian mss. The members of most classes show further common features, only the most obvious of which are given here. Statements on the use of vowel signs in table I and in this paper generally are not absolute, but general, i.e. mss classed as using ⟨a⟩ where bA has *qameṣ* may also use ⟨a′⟩, but only in a small percentage of cases. The numbers across the top of table I indicate the following:

i Where bA uses *qameṣ ḥaṭuf* Pal. uses . . .
ii ” ” ” *ḥaṭef qameṣ* ” ”
iii ” ” ” *qameṣ* ” ”
iv ” ” ” *pataḥ* ” ”
v ” ” ” *segol* ” ”
vi ” ” ” *ṣere* ” ”
vii ” ” ” *shewa*[10] ” ”
viii Number of biblical texts of this class known.
ix Number of non-biblical texts of this class known.

The numbers down the side of the table indicate the classes of Palestinian mss.[11]

TABLE I

	i	ii	iii	iv	v	vi	vii	viii	ix
1	⟨o/a⟩	⟨a⟩	⟨a⟩	⟨a′⟩	⟨e⟩	⟨e′⟩	⟨e⟩	3	5
2	⟨o/a/a′⟩	⟨a/a′⟩	⟨a⟩	⟨a′⟩	⟨e/e′⟩	⟨e/e′⟩	⟨a′/e⟩	3	10
3	⟨o/a/a′⟩	⟨a′⟩[12]	⟨a/a′⟩	⟨a/a′⟩	⟨e/e′⟩	⟨e/e′⟩	⟨a′/e/e′⟩	5	6
4	⟨o⟩	⟨a⟩	⟨a⟩	⟨a′⟩	⟨e⟩		⟨e′/a′⟩	–	5
5	⟨o/a/a′⟩	⟨a/a′⟩	⟨a/a′⟩	⟨a/a′⟩	⟨e⟩		⟨e′/a′⟩	–	4
6	⟨o⟩	⟨a⟩	⟨a⟩	⟨a′⟩	⟨e⟩		–	–	7
7	⟨o/a/a′⟩	–	⟨a/a′⟩	⟨a/a′⟩	⟨e⟩		⟨a′/e⟩	4	12
8	⟨o⟩	⟨a⟩	⟨a⟩		⟨e⟩		⟨a′⟩	–	1
9	⟨o⟩	⟨a⟩	⟨a⟩		⟨e⟩		⟨e⟩	–	6
10	–	–	⟨a⟩		⟨e′⟩		⟨e′⟩	–	3
11	⟨o⟩	–	⟨a′⟩		⟨e⟩		⟨a′/e⟩	–	2

9 Under the title *Hebrew Texts with Palestinian Vocalization* by the University of Toronto Press. This study, which owes much to Dr. Dietrich (see appendix A), is referred to here as HTPV.

10 Special cases, such as the use of ⟨i⟩ where bA has *shewa* before *yod*, are not included here.

11 Examples of mss. of the various classes are: cl. 1, Bod. Heb. e30 f. 48–9+, TS H16:10; cl. 2, Bod. Heb. d44 f. 1–4+, TS H16:7; cl. 3, TS 12:195+, Ant. 959; cl. 4, TS H16:4; cl. 5, TS H16:8; cl. 6, TS H2:30; cl. 7, Bod. Heb. d29 f. 17–20, TS H16:3+; cl. 8, TS NS 249:14+; cl. 9, TS H7:1; cl. 10, TS NS 117:7+; cl. 11, TS H2:29.

12 One example only.

4 The following points can be established from this table.

(i) Mss. of class 1, those in which the Palestinian use of signs is most similar to that of bA, form a very small proportion of the total number of known mss. It is therefore unlikely that they represent the standard form of Palestinian pointing, of which all others are the work of an ignorant copyist.[13]

(ii) Members of classes 8–11, which use only one 'a' sign and one 'e' sign, form an almost equally small proportion of the known mss. It is therefore unlikely that the Palestinian dialect in general should be credited with only one 'a' and one 'e' vowel on the basis of these texts.

(iii) Mss. of classes 1, 2, 4, and 6 use ⟨a⟩ and ⟨a′⟩ much as bA uses *qameṣ* and *pataḥ*. Mss. of classes 2, 4, and 6 do not show any other features likely to have derived from bA influence, in fact rather the reverse (see (iv) below). There is, therefore, no reason to suppose that the use of ⟨a⟩ and ⟨a′⟩ in this way is not a genuinely native feature of some types of Palestinian Hebrew (compare classes 3, 5, and 7 with 2, 4, and 6). Consequently the history of Palestinian Hebrew cannot have been one of unilinear development from the use of two 'a' and 'e' signs to the use of four, and from 'non-bA' to 'bA type' use of these signs.

(iv) Apart from mss. of class 1 (in which it is perhaps due to bA influence), the use of ⟨a⟩ where bA has *qameṣ ḥaṭuf* is confined to mss. of classes 5 and 7, in which the use of the 'a' signs is quite different from that of bA, and to mss. of class 2, which shows many similarities to them. The use of ⟨a′⟩ where bA has *qameṣ ḥaṭuf* or *ḥaṭef qameṣ* is found only in these mss. Texts of classes 4 and 6, in which the 'a' signs are otherwise used as are those of bA, use ⟨o⟩ where bA has *qameṣ ḥaṭuf*, and ⟨a⟩ where bA has *ḥaṭef qameṣ*. The use of ⟨a⟩ where bA has *qameṣ ḥaṭuf* is not, therefore, a mark of bA influence, but derives from the Palestinian traditions most different from bA. These four points, then, show that the views cited in paragraph 2 are all unsatisfactory.

5 Scholars appear to be unanimous in their opinion that Pal. represents a stage of the language earlier than that recorded in bA.

13 There are, in any case, numerous dissimilarities between mss. of class 1 and bA, of which the most important is the absence of a special sign for '*shewa* vowels' in Pal. texts (see below § II.15). In my opinion, the use of ⟨a⟩ where bA has *qameṣ ḥaṭuf* is the only likely example of 'Tiberianization' in these mss. (see (iii) below and HTPV III.1 and IV.1).

While various suggestions have been put forward to account for the number and use of the vowel signs, however, there has never been a serious attempt to place the Palestinian forms in the chain of Hebrew morphological development.[14] For instance, both Origen's transliterations and bA clearly distinguish two signs for 'e' vowels. The majority of Palestinian mss. do not. Palestinian Hebrew, even in classes 3, 5, and 7, is clearly in the same line of development as are Origen's transliterations and bA.[15] Are we, then, to postulate the complete loss and revival of a distinction between two 'e' vowels in the period between the production of Origen's transliterations and bA? No clear answer has ever been suggested for this and the many similar questions which could be raised. The present paper is an attempt to supply answers by determining the place of Palestinian Hebrew in the history of the language on the basis of its use of vowel signs.

6 All Palestinian mss. known to me in 1965 have been used as sources for this study. All mss. are quoted by their library number. References to biblical mss. are to biblical chapter and verse. References to non-biblical mss. are to f(olio) (where applicable), r(ecto) or v(erso), and line. The practice of former editors is too diverse to permit their systems of line numbering to be used without confusion. Where line numbering in a published text is not that of the ms., numbers are given in parentheses after the first reference, indicating the *page* and *line* of the published edition. This system is also used for the Leningrad texts of which I have not yet been able to get photographs. The place of publication of all published texts is given in appendix A. This list also includes all texts referred to in this article.[16] Because fuller information will be available in a subsequent publication, few examples have been given here. Palestinian Hebrew, where possible, is quoted in graphemic transcription.[17] bA Hebrew, quoted for comparison, is also given in the form of

14 Ben David (1958) does argue at length on the date of Palestinian Hebrew, but makes no attempt to solve the problems his view raises, or even the apparent conflict in his own statements (see paragraph 34).

15 The many similarities which can be seen between the transliterations of Origen and bA (see Brønno, 1943, p. 462), between the transliterations of Origen and Pal. (see Sperber, 1938, pp. 144f.), and between bA and Pal. (see ben David, 1958, p. 483) show this. Babylonian Hebrew, as pointed out by ben David there, is in a different line of development.

16 A complete list of the texts used for this study appears in HTPV.

17 Transcription of consonants is conventional, and that of vowel signs is given in paragraph 2 above. These letters are placed within 'pointed brackets' ⟨⟩ to indicate graphemic transcription.

transcribed graphemes, but in italics to avoid confusion.[18] Attempted phonetic or phonemic transcription is deliberately avoided for reasons which, in the grammatical study of written texts, should be obvious.[19]

The 'indiscriminate' use of 'a' and 'e' signs in Palestinian texts

7 When the Palestinian use of vowel signs is compared to that of bA, the most obvious Palestinian characteristic is the apparent confusion in the use of the 'a' signs (classes 3, 5, and 7) and the 'e' signs (classes 2 and 3). It is usually said that the mss. of these classes use these signs 'indiscriminately.' There is, however, reason to believe that ⟨a⟩ and ⟨a'⟩, and ⟨e⟩ and ⟨e'⟩, were to some extent distinguished in these mss., although the distinction was different from that made by bA in the use of *qameṣ*, *pataḥ*, *segol*, and *ṣere*. In order to determine the Palestinian use of the four 'a' and 'e' signs, the texts of these classes were analysed into their component morphs.[20] This was done first in the biblical mss. Each morph containing an 'a' or 'e' sign was listed. Any morph which occurred frequently, and in which the same 'a' or 'e' sign was regularly used, was noted, and these morphs only were studied in non-biblical texts. This method was used to reduce the material to manageable proportions. It should, however, be noted that morphs regularly written with a particular 'a' or 'e' sign in non-biblical texts may be

18 The system used is that of Schramm, 1964, no. 2.4 (pp. 7–8) save that stress position is not normally indicated.

19 Either type of transcription applied even to such a relatively well-documented form of Hebrew as bA must remain highly questionable, as can be seen from a comparison of the various attempts to reconstruct the bA phoneme system. Even the consonantal system is uncertain. This makes a highly unsatisfactory basis for grammatical study. Graphemes and phonemes can be considered as parallel methods of representing morphemes (see McIntosh, 1956, especially p. 40), and should be so considered in the grammatical study of written texts. The use of the term 'phoneme' in the study of such texts is a ludicrous contradiction of its meaning, and (since the value of a scientific term of this sort is that it represents a single category) a dangerous perversion of the idea it stands for. If enough information exists, an attempt can be made to designate the sounds indicated by the graphemes, but this should be done only on the basis of a complete study of the graphemic system.

20 This is the only way in the use of the signs by the Palestinians themselves can be checked. The mere existence of pairs of identical forms in which two different signs are used indiscriminately is not a valid indicator. It is true of bA (see Sperber, 1959, pp. 35f. for examples). Nor is a comparison of the Pal. use of signs to that of bA any indication of what is regular in Pal. However if, in Pal., either one of two signs is commonly used to write a particular morph in a particular grammatical context, they may truly be said to be used indiscriminately – and vice versa.

infrequent or non-existent in the biblical texts available, and would therefore not be included in this study. The number of morphs noted here is not, therefore, necessarily any indication of the number in which regularity of vowel sign use is found. In order to cut down the amount of material, few unpublished texts were used in the study of the 'a' signs, for which there is plenty of information. As many texts as possible were used in the study of the 'e' signs. A list of the texts used for this study, and comparative data on their use of the 'a' and 'e' signs, is given in appendix B.

8 The most obvious evidence for the existence, within the mss. studied, of a distinction between ⟨a⟩ and ⟨a′⟩ is to be seen in the bound forms of the second person masculine singular pronoun. The 'pronominal suffix' (bA *-kɔ*) is normally (over 90%) written with ⟨a⟩. In biblical texts, only two exceptions occur in 71 examples. Even in these cases the horizontal stroke may represent an accent, not ⟨a′⟩.[21] This morph is rare in non-biblical texts (see paragraph 38), where it is usually written with ⟨a′⟩. The allomorph common in non-biblical texts (bA *-ɔk*) shows no orthographic regularity.[22] The pronoun in the second person masculine singular perfect verb form (bA *-tɔ*) shows usage similar to *-kɔ*. In biblical and rabbinic texts it is usually written with ⟨a⟩.[23] In liturgical texts, it is often written with ⟨a′⟩, but usage varies according to the ms.[24] These *-kɔ* and *-tɔ* forms, then, do give examples of the distinctive use of the 'a' signs in a genuine Palestinian situation, even if only in biblical texts.[25]

9 Table II shows further morphs in which a high degree of uniformity in the use of 'a' signs obtains, both in biblical and non-biblical texts. The statistics on the *pi'el* are given to provide cases of

21 The exceptions are both in Bod. Heb. d29 f. 17–20, Josh. 17:15, 17. Hand A's accents were changed by later hands elsewhere: e.g. Josh. 18:20.

22 There is, however, considerable regularity in certain contexts; thus, when bound to the 'inseparable prepositions,' this morph is usually written with ⟨a⟩.

23 In 34 examples there are four exceptions, all in TS NS 249:3.

24 Thus in Bod. ms. Heb. d41 f. 15v, 15r 1–15, ⟨a⟩ is used 16 times, ⟨a′⟩ once. In TS H16:8, ⟨a⟩ is used twice, ⟨a′⟩ 18 times.

25 It might be argued, because of the theories which have been built on these morphs, that *-kɔ* and *-tɔ* do not represent the 'true' Palestinian dialect. My own opinion on this is given in paragraph 38, but the question is not relevant here. The point which must be made here is that, even if the consonant plus vowel form of these suffixes did derive from outside influence, there is no reason why the vowel should not be represented indiscriminately by ⟨a⟩ or ⟨a′⟩. This is, in fact, the case with the vowel plus consonant form, even where it appears in biblical mss. There is no other sign, in the mss. in which the spelling of *-kɔ* and *-tɔ* was studied, of any thoroughgoing attempt to use ⟨a⟩ as bA uses *qameṣ*.

completely indiscriminate use to contrast with the discrimination exercised in the spelling of the other forms given.

TABLE II

Morph	bA form	Use of ⟨a⟩	Use of ⟨a'⟩
3ms. pron. bound to pl. nouns	*-ɔyw*	2	110
3fs. pron. in perfect verb forms	*-ɔh*	50	8
1cs. pron. bound to pl. nouns	*-ay/ɔy*	8	52
Preposition (free form)	*ʿal*	85	13
Perfect *qal* (first syllable)	*qɔ(tal)*, etc.	260	65
Imperfect *nifʿal*	*yiqqɔtel*, etc.	50	3
Infinitive construct *piʿel*	*qattel*	34	26
Imperative *piʿel*	*qattel*, etc.	31	39

10 The most interesting, and probably the most important, evidence for the distinction of ⟨e⟩ and ⟨e'⟩ is found in the 'segolate' nouns. The use of vowel signs in such nouns and similar forms can be tabulated as in table III.

TABLE III

	Biblical		Non-biblical	
	⟨e⟩	⟨e'⟩	⟨e⟩	⟨e'⟩
In the first syllable				
bA *qéṭɛl/qétɛl*	57	9	35	9
bA nouns ending *-élɛt*	–	2	8	6
bA segolate infinitives	–	1	–	–
In the second syllable				
bA *qóṭɛl*	4	2	2	2
bA *qɔ́ṭɛl*	7	2	–	1
bA *qéṭɛl/qétɛl*	5	17	18	5
bA nouns ending *-ólɛt*	–	–	–	3
bA nouns ending *-élɛt*	–	3	11	4
bA segolate infinitives	–	1	–	1

11 Table III shows that, in biblical mss., ⟨e⟩ is normally used in the first syllable of segolate forms. In the second syllable, after 'e' vowels, ⟨e'⟩ is normally used. Of the five exceptions, three are from TS 20:53+, a text which shows many differences in pointing from typical Palestinian texts, and the other two are from TS 12:195+.[26] If the first syllable of a segolate form contains an 'a' or an 'o' sign, ⟨e⟩ is normally used in the second. Of the four exceptions,

26 See TS 20:53+, Pss. 32:6, 7, 35:19 (the latter instance is only given in the edition of Allony and Díez-Macho, 1958*a*); TS 12:195+, Pss. 52:10, 72:2.

three are from TS 20:53+.[27] The use of ⟨e⟩ in the second syllable of these forms thus appears to be connected with, and is therefore presumably dependent on, the presence of an 'a' or 'o' vowel in the preceding syllable. It is most surprising to find that the use of ⟨e′⟩ in the first syllable apparently depends on similar conditions. Of the 12 cases in which ⟨e′⟩ is used in this position, 8 would follow 'a' or 'o' vowels.[28] The same change of ⟨e⟩ to ⟨e′⟩ can be seen in similar situations in other forms.[29] If, then, both the use of ⟨e⟩ in the second syllable and of ⟨e′⟩ in the first are due to grammatical (presumably phonological) conditions, these biblical texts show 76 per cent regular spelling in the final syllable,[30] and 96 per cent regularity in the first syllable.[31] The non-biblical texts do not normally use ⟨e′⟩ in the final syllable, nor do they follow the sign changes after 'a' or 'o' vowels noted in the biblical texts. They use ⟨e⟩ in the first syllable with about 80 per cent regularity.

12 Table IV shows other morphs showing regularity in their use of 'e' signs in both biblical and non-biblical texts. This information could have been augmented if morphs for which fewer than 10 examples were found were listed. The last item is included to con-

TABLE IV

Morph	bA form	Use of ⟨e⟩	Use of ⟨e′⟩
Inseparable prepositions	*bə-*, etc.[32]	51	6
Preposition	*me-*	22	–
Particle	*'eyn*	11	1
Imperf. *qal* of initial weak verbs	*yɛhĕtal*, etc.	10	–
Perf. and partic. *nif'al* of initial weak verbs	*nɛhĕtal*, etc.	16	1
Participle *qal*	*qotel*	17	17

27 See TS 20:53+, Pss. 35:26, 37:25, 29; the fourth case is TS 12:195+, Ps. 74:17.

28 It should be noted that the use of ⟨e′⟩ in this position has no connection with philological **qitl*. The cases are: J.T.S. ms. 594, Eccles. 11:6; TS 20:53+, Pss. 30:5, 32:6, 8, 37:34, 39:7, 40:5; TS 20:59+, Ezek. 1:7, 13, 14:21, 16:6; TS NS 249:8+, Judg. 6:3.

29 Thus TS 12:195+ uses ⟨e⟩ in bA *'el* (Pss. 52:3, 77:10) but ⟨e′⟩ in bA *hɔ'el* (Ps. 77:15); so also TS 20:59 uses ⟨e⟩ in bA *mɛšiy* (Ezek. 16:10) but ⟨e′⟩ in bA *wɔmɛšiy* (Ezek. 16:13). See also note 70.

30 I.e. 21 regular uses of ⟨e′⟩, and 11 of ⟨e⟩, from a total of 42 examples.

31 I.e. 57 regular uses of ⟨e⟩, and 8 of ⟨e′⟩, from a total of 69 examples.

32 'a' signs are also used in this position, relatively rarely in bliblical mss. but more commonly in non-biblical. It is a peculiarity of many of these mss. that, where 'e' vowels are used in positions where bA uses *shewa*, ⟨e⟩ is more commonly used in the first syllable of a word, but ⟨e′⟩ in medial syllables.

trast with more regular morphs, and also with the second vowel of 'segolate' forms with 'o' vowel. A final indication of distinction of the two signs is that ⟨e⟩ is regularly used where bA has *ḥaṭef segol* while the use of ⟨e′⟩ in this position is so rare as to be negligible.

13 This information clearly shows that there is a partial distinction in use between ⟨a⟩ and ⟨a′⟩, and between ⟨e⟩ and ⟨e′⟩, in the texts where these signs are normally said to be used 'indiscriminately.' The evidence may not seem very impressive, but it shows usage regular throughout this stratum of Palestinian Hebrew. Smaller groups of mss. would show a higher degree of uniformity. It seems clear that, over the whole group of texts of this type, some morphs were normally (over 80% of the cases) written with a single 'a' or 'e' sign, while others were written with either of the two 'a' signs or the two 'e' signs indiscriminately. If ⟨a⟩, ⟨a′⟩,⟨e⟩, and ⟨e′⟩ are equated to *qameṣ*, *pataḥ*, *segol*, and *ṣere*, it will be seen that the Palestinian spelling of the morphs in which regularity of sign usage is maintained does not always correspond to that of bA. This is, then, a genuinely Palestinian distinction.

14 The distinction, when it was made, was almost certainly one of vowel quality. It is not likely to have been purely orthographic, as uniformity does not necessarily occur in the same orthographic situation.[33] It is not likely to have been a distinction of vowel quantity, as any of the four 'a' and 'e' signs can stand in any type of syllable corresponding to all quantities of bA vowels from *shewa* to 'full vowel' under main stress.[34] We are, then, left with vowel quality as the most likely basis for distinction. This is, indeed, what the study of the other Hebrew vocalization systems would lead us to expect.[35] This suggestion is supported by the fact that, in biblical

33 For instance, the pronominal element in the third person feminine singular verb form is regularly written with ⟨a⟩ (see paragraph 9), but the ending of feminine noun forms, or the emphatic ending of imperfect and imperative verb forms, both of which are also written *-ɔh* in bA, show no regularity of orthography in Pal.

34 Some scholars will deny that this has any significance for the quantity of Palestinian vowels (cf. Sperber, 1959, p. 77). However, it is ludicrous to maintain that differences in quantity did not exist merely because different signs were not used. Such an argument would make simple and complex Babylonian texts or written and spoken English representative of different dialects. The existence of '*shewa* vowels' in Palestinian Hebrew is demonstrated in § 11 of this study.

35 The basic intention of both the Tiberian and the Babylonian styles of pointing is to indicate vowel quality. The simple *shewa* sign is an exception in both systems. In general, however, indication of quantity ('composite' *shewa* signs, complex system) is secondary, and is omitted from many mss. in both styles. See the assessment of these styles in Morag, 1962.

mss. at least, the 'e' vowels of 'segolate' nouns appear to be influenced by the preceding vowel (see paragraph 10). A change produced by a particular vowel quality is likely to be a change in quality. From the use of the Palestinian signs, we can reasonably suggest that the sounds represented by ⟨a⟩, ⟨a'⟩, ⟨e⟩, and ⟨e'⟩ were similar to those represented by *qameṣ*, *pataḥ*, *segol*, and *ṣere* respectively. Any attempt at further precision would be of little value.

The interchange of vowel signs in Palestinian texts

15 In general, it can be said that the Palestinian vowel signs correspond to those of bA as follows: ⟨u⟩ to *shureq*, ⟨o⟩ to *ḥolem*, ⟨a⟩ to *qameṣ*, ⟨a'⟩ to *pataḥ*, ⟨e⟩ to *segol*, ⟨e'⟩ to *ṣere*, ⟨i⟩ to *ḥireq*.[36] Apart from the interchanges of 'a' signs and of 'e' signs just described, however, Palestinian mss. show certain characteristic divergences from this typical use of the signs. These divergences may be held to represent the characteristic differences of Palestinian Hebrew from that of bA. If these divergent uses are listed according to the situations in which they occur, several different 'patterns of occurrence' appear. Thus some changes are virtually restricted to closed, unstressed syllables, some to closed, stressed syllables, and so on. Since bA and Pal. represent dialects in the same general stream of development (see note 15) these patterns of change may be expected to indicate the process by which the differences between the two dialects were produced. The various interchanges of vowel signs are considered below according to the 'patterns of occurrence' which they show. In order to clarify matters, only the main features of the patterns are considered in the body of this paper. Exact details of the major divergent uses of vowel signs are given in appendix C.

16 *Pattern 1* Changes taking place in stressed[37] syllables, or in unstressed syllables before a laryngeal or a doubled consonant.

36 Pal. has no single sign which corresponds to bA *shewa*. For the signs used where bA has *shewa* see paragraph 3 above, and § 11 of this article.

37 Note that the term 'stressed' refers to syllables stressed in bA. It is not suggested that the stress pattern of the Palestinian dialect was necessarily the same.

	STRESSED		UNSTRESSED, BEFORE	
	Closed	Open	Laryngeal	Doubled consonant
⟨o⟩ = *shureq*	xx[38]	xx	x	xx
⟨a⟩ = *pataḥ*	xx	–	x	x
⟨e⟩ = *pataḥ*	–	–	xx	–
⟨e/e′⟩ = *ḥireq*	xx	x	xx	xx

(also ⟨e′⟩ = *segol*? See paragraph 28)

The changes showing this pattern all represent changes of vowel quality induced by stress position and loss of syllable closure. This is the type of change called 'stress lengthening' or 'compensatory lengthening' in traditional grammars of bA. The same changes have occurred in other positions in the stage of Hebrew recorded by bA.[39] The evidence in Pal., then, would appear to indicate that a vowel change, which has taken place in certain situations in bA and in Pal., is taking place in Pal. under similar conditions in new situations.

17 ⟨o⟩ = *shureq*. The change 'u → o' in open, stressed syllables is commonly assumed to have taken place in many situations in Hebrew before the stage recorded by bA, e.g. **ʾuzn* → *ʾózɛn*. The same change occurred before certain laryngeals: e.g. *yəquttal*, but *yəborak*. It also occurred in closed, final stressed syllables: e.g. *kullow*, but *kol*. The last two examples show the change occurring as the result of the loss of original doubling of a consonant. The use of ⟨o⟩ where ⟨u⟩ is expected occurs in Pal. under similar conditions. The occurrences before laryngeals are usually in so-called virtually closed syllables. This shows the obvious continuation of a process **ruḥḥaṣti* → bA *ruḥaṣtə* → Pal. ⟨roḥaṣt⟩ identical with the one which produced the 'o' vowel in bA *puʿal* forms with medial *resh* or *ʾalef*.[40] Cases where this change occurs in Pal. before a consonant which could be doubled in bA suggest that the consonant is not doubled in Pal. It is hardly surprising to find that this loss of ability to double consonants, which is well attested for some con-

38 ⟨o⟩ = *shureq* is to be read 'Pal. has ⟨o⟩ where bA uses *shureq*'; 'xx' indicates that a change occurs commonly and 'x,' fairly commonly.

39 This statement is based on the assumption that the Pal. vowel signs indicate more or less the same sounds as do the corresponding (see paragraph 15 above) signs in bA. This assumption is fully justified by the fact that the number of cases in which, for example, ⟨u⟩ corresponds to bA *shureq* is vastly greater than the number of cases in which it does not. For the 'a' and 'e' vowels, see paragraph 14.

40 Examples of this change are המרוחק H.U.C. ms. 1001, 1r21; זועמו Ant. 369, 2r30 (19:16); רחצת TS 20:59, Ezek. 16:4.

sonants and some positions in bA,[41] should have spread to other positions and other consonants in Pal.[42] It is more surprising to one reared on the traditional terminology to find that so-called pure long vowels in stressed final syllables have changed. The same change of quality has, however, taken place in other positions in bA.[43] It is to be expected that it should spread to new situations.[44]

18 ⟨a⟩ = *pataḥ*. The change corresponding to this in bA (*pataḥ* → *qameṣ*) is so common as to need no description. The Palestinian change occurs in the same situations as does that of 'u → o,' with the exception of open final syllables, where *pataḥ* does not occur. The change may be ascribed to the same causes which produce the change of *pataḥ* to *qameṣ* in bA,[45] and (apparently) the change ⟨u⟩ → ⟨o⟩ in Pal.: the effect of stress alone in stressed syllables, and the effect of (secondary) stress combined with loss of closure in 'unstressed' syllables.[46] Since the syllables which have changed in bA have also changed in Pal., but many of those which have changed in Pal. have not changed in bA, it is logical to conclude that Pal. represents a stage of the language later than that recorded in bA. The information used here is taken only from mss. of classes 1, 2, 4, and 6, which use their 'a' signs almost exactly as bA uses *qameṣ*

41 E.g. laryngeals; *waw*, *yod*, *lamed*, *mem*, *nun*, *qof*, and others, before *shewa*; any consonant in word final position.

42 E.g. חקך TS 20:59+, Ezek. 16:27; בארבות J.T.S. ms. 594, Eccles. 12:3; לעומת Ant. 912, p. 25, l. 9.

43 Even under stress, in forms such as *tɔšobnɔ* (at least if "*ayin waw*' verbs did originally have as 'root' a long 'u' vowel between two consonants).

44 E.g. זבל TS NS 281:2 (4 times); חמץ Bod. Heb. d63 f. 88b10; תאבו Ant. 369, 2r22 (19:8); הוא TS H16:1 r13 (29:8). It is possible that the interchanges of ⟨o⟩ and ⟨u⟩ found in Pal. (see also paragraphs 22, 28) should be considered as symptomatic of a general loss of distinction between 'o' and 'u' vowels, such as evidently occurred in the Samaritan pronunciation of Hebrew, and perhaps even in the pronunciation recorded in TS 20:53+. However, in view of the fact that the patterns of occurrence shown by these changes are paralleled by those of other changes, I think this unlikely. It seems to me even more unlikely that Murtonen could be right in his view that the use of one sign (⟨o⟩) in TS 20:53+ where most mss. use ⟨o⟩ and ⟨u⟩ reflects 'earlier times' (Murtonen, 1958, p. 32), since there is no reason to suppose that 'o' and 'u' vowels were not distinct in Hebrew from its earliest beginnings. If he is referring to graphic rather than phonemic distinction, this is found in Origen's transliterations, and could surely have been re-invented, if necessary, by any Jewish scholar.

45 This need hardly be argued in the case of closed, stressed, final syllables. The fact that bA retains *pataḥ* in some of these is always a stumbling-block to historical grammarians.

46 Three stress levels can easily be distinguished in bA in open syllables: primary ('tone'), secondary (conventionally called 'pretonic' although it frequently occurs elsewhere, as in *qɔ̀təlɔ́*), and tertiary (on syllables containing '*shewa* vowels').

and *pataḥ*. It would seem that these mss. record a situation in which the ‘a’ vowel system as recorded in bA is undergoing further change, while those studied in paragraphs 8 and 9 record a situation in which the distinction between two ‘a’ vowels has largely broken down.[47]

19 ⟨e⟩ = *pataḥ*. The corresponding change in bA (*pataḥ* → *segol*) would not normally be connected with that of *pataḥ* to *qameṣ*. Nevertheless, *segol* often represents an intermediate stage in that change.[48] The use of ⟨e⟩ in Pal. where bA uses *pataḥ* undoubtedly represents a similar change. It occurs almost solely in connection with laryngeals, and far more commonly before a laryngeal than in any other position.[49] This change, then, undoubtedly represents, in most cases where it occurs, a change in vowel quality due to a following laryngeal. Ben David’s ascription of examples of this change to a residual general confusion of ‘a’ and ‘e’ vowels, indicating connection with the Babylonian dialect of Hebrew, is to be rejected.[50]

47 Examples of this change are: מלך TS K26:8, II Kings 8:16; נתתיך TS 12:197, Jer. 1:5; רחק TS H16:4, r18. Besides the positions listed in paragraph 16, this change also occurs in fairly large numbers in unstressed syllables, both open and closed, probably as the result of confusion (cf. paragraphs 27, 28).

48 Original short ‘a’ appears as *segol* under the influence of *qameṣ* (*’aḥiym* but *’ɛḥɔyw ‘ad* but *wɔ‘ɛd*, the article pointed with *segol*, etc.) and in some open, stressed syllables (**malk* → *mɛ́lɛk*). In many similar cases the change to *qameṣ* has already been completed (*hɔhɔ́r*, but cf. *hɛhɔríym*). For further examples, see Gesenius-Kautzch, 1910, no. 27q, r.

49 Thus: before a laryngeal, medial, 18 cases, e.g. יחדו TS 12:195+, Ps. 71:10; ותעדי TS 20:59+, Ezek. 16:13; בעלי Bod. Heb. d63 f. 82r28; final, 13 cases, e.g. קלע Ant. 369, 2r8 (18:11); קדח Bod. Heb. d55 f. 10r5, מלח Bod. Heb. d63 f. 88v15. Elsewhere it is common only in closed, unstressed syllables; 10 of its 13 uses in this position follow laryngeals, and are probably due to their influence, e.g. ענוות Bod. Heb. d55 f. 4r8, etc.; הדרתך *ibid.* 5v10, etc.

50 See ben David, 1958, p. 490. Various grounds for rejection besides the explanation given above can be supplied. The change is not general, but occurs in specific situations. Furthermore, the sign עַ̱, used in Bab. in many of the cases in which bA uses *segol* (but by no means all; see note 3), represents an ‘a’ vowel, not an ‘e’ vowel. This is shown (i) by the morphs in which this sign is not used where bA has *segol*, (ii) by the fact that ‘Tiberianizing’ Bab. mss. make the six basic Bab. signs up to seven by creating a new sign to correspond to *segol*, not *pataḥ* (Kahle, 1913, mss. 7a, b, c; 36, 38c, 40c), (iii) by the form of the new sign in ms. 7 there; עֱ presumably indicates ‘a’ coloured by ‘e.’ Consequently, if Pal. reflected the same pronunciation as is recorded in Bab., we would find an ‘e’ vowel replaced by an ‘a’ vowel, not the other way about. ⟨a′⟩ = *segol* is rare in Pal. (see appendix c). For ⟨e⟩ and ⟨e′⟩ = *ḥaṭef pataḥ*, also included in ben David’s argument, see paragraph 36.

20 ⟨e/e′⟩ = *ḥireq*. The change corresponding to this in bA (*ḥireq* → *ṣere*) represents another well-known change in vowel quality produced under the same effects of stress and loss of syllable closure as the change *pataḥ* → *qameṣ* (see 18). The Palestinian use of ⟨ e⟩ or ⟨e′⟩ where bA has *ḥireq* occurs in the same positions as ⟨o⟩ = *shureq* and ⟨a⟩ = *pataḥ*, and can be interpreted in the same way. A change which has already taken place in some positions in bA is found in Pal. in those positions, and also in positions which are new, but related to those in which the change has already occurred.[51] This shows that a process which was in progress in bA has progressed further in Pal. ⟨e⟩ = *ḥireq* is much more common than ⟨e′⟩ = *ḥireq*. This is probably due simply to the fact that ⟨e⟩ is used very much more frequently than ⟨e′⟩, even in mss. which use both (see appendix B).

21 *Pattern 2* Changes taking place in an open, unstressed syllable.

		STRESSED		UNSTRESSSED
	Closed	Open final	Open	Open
⟨u⟩ = *ḥolem*	x	x	–	xx
⟨e/e′⟩ = *qameṣ*	–	–	–	xx
⟨a′⟩ = *qameṣ*	(xx)	(x)	–	xx
⟨i⟩ = *ṣere*	x	–	x	xx
(⟨e⟩ = *ṣere*	x	x	–	(x))

These changes also represent a change in vowel quality induced by the stress pattern. In this case, however, they are due to the removal or weakening of stress; the type of change is called 'reduction' in traditional terminology. This interpretation is unquestionable in the case of ⟨e/e′⟩ = *qameṣ*. The other cases are not so clear, and must be interpreted with the help of this one.

22 ⟨u⟩ = *ḥolem*. This change takes place most commonly in unstressed, open syllables, where it can be interpreted, by comparison with the change described in 23 below, as a change caused by weakening of syllable stress, the opposite of that described in 17.[52] This is not to be understood mechanically. The situation

51 Examples are: דודים TS 20:59+, Ezek. 16:8; להשמין TS H16:6, 1v16 (2:19); לוי Bod. Heb. d55 f. 14r14; מי TS 20:53+, Ps. 39:7; וויעוד TS H16:6, 1v1 (2:4); איחרו TS 13H2:10, 2v2; איבנה *ibid.* 2r15; האדרש TS 20:59+, Ezek. 14:3. On examples of this change occurring in closed, unstressed syllables, see paragraph 27.

52 E.g. מותרת TS H16:7, 2r29 (22:18); נפשותינו Bod. Heb. d55 f. 10v33; קוממיות Bod. Heb. d41 f. 15v5 (43:8).

envisaged is that an original 'u' sound, under the conditions described in 17, was realized as an 'o' sound and written ⟨o⟩. When an 'o' vowel which had been produced under these conditions was pronounced under weaker stress, the sound realized was regarded by the Palestinians as closer to 'u' than to 'o,' and written accordingly.[53] The same change occurs in stressed syllables, where it is no doubt to be ascribed to different causes.[54]

23 ⟨e/e′⟩ = *qameṣ*. This phenomenon occurs in the case of ⟨e⟩ almost only, and in the case of ⟨e′⟩ only, in open, unstressed syllables. The use of ⟨e′⟩ is common only in mss. of classes 4 and 5. In these classes ⟨e′⟩ is used almost solely where bA has *shewa*.[55] Similarly, in the mss. in which ⟨e⟩ = *qameṣ* occurs, ⟨e⟩ is frequently used where bA has *shewa*. Consequently it seems certain that, in these cases of ⟨e/e′⟩ = *qameṣ*, the vowel represented in bA by *qameṣ* has been replaced in the Palestinian dialect by a vowel of *shewa* quantity. This is presumably due to some change in the stress pattern which caused a weakening of the stress on the syllables in question. This must be a change which took place after the stage of the language recorded by bA. It cannot be taken as an indication that 'pretonal lengthening' had not yet taken place because this had already occurred by the time of Origen's transcriptions.[56] Furthermore, it would be impossible to explain the use of ⟨e′⟩ as the representative of an 'a' sound which had not undergone 'pretonal lengthening.'

24 ⟨a′⟩ = *qameṣ*. The statistics given here are taken only from mss. of classes 1, 2, 4, and 6, which use ⟨a⟩ and ⟨a′⟩ much as bA uses *qameṣ* and *pataḥ*. The information provided shows 38 examples of this change in open, unstressed syllables. These are to be

53 The type of change involved is shown in the vowel represented by 'e' in Southern British 'parliament' /pā́ləmənt/, 'parliamentary' /pā̀limέntriy/, and 'parliamentarian' /pā̀ləməntέriyən/. Cf. also Bauer-Leander, 1922, no. 14q.

54 See paragraph 28. It is also possible that a number of cases of ⟨u⟩ = *ḥolem* are due simply to the absence of the top dot of the ⟨o⟩ sign, either through scribal carelessness or through deterioration of the ms.

55 ⟨e′⟩ is used in class 4 = *qameṣ*, 4 cases; = *segol* or *ḥaṭef segol*, 3 cases (in נעשקה TS 13H2:10, 2v23, and two similar forms, all of which could be 'pausal'); = *ḥaṭef pataḥ*, 4 cases; = simple *shewa*, 79 cases. In class 5 = *qameṣ*, 3 cases; = *pataḥ*, 1 case; = *segol*, 2 cases; = *ḥireq*, 1 case; = *ḥaṭef pataḥ*, 14 cases; = *ḥaṭef segol*, 1 case; = simple *shewa*, 93 cases.

56 See Brønno, 1943, p. 156. Examples of the change are: יבאו TS 12:195+, Ps. 69:28; השע TS 20:53+, Ps. 39:14; מישגבו Bod. Heb. d55 f. 13v23; השיבו TS 20:59+, Ezek. 14:6; ימין TS H16:4, r10; מלחמות TS 13H2:10, 1r2.

interpreted in the same way as the other changes showing pattern 2.[57] The weakening of the stress on the syllables showing this change had not progressed far enough for the Palestinian scholars to note the sound as of *shewa* quantity as in the cases described in 23 above. Change had begun, however, so that the vowel in question was closer to those represented by ⟨a′⟩ than to those represented by ⟨a⟩, and was written accordingly. Many examples of this change also occur in stressed syllables (see paragraph 28).

25 ⟨i⟩ = *ṣere*. This change is assumed to represent the same type of vowel change by loss of stress as is described in 23.[58] The use of ⟨i⟩ to represent the resulting sound is not to be seen specifically as a return to the original vowel sound, but merely as the closest approximation to a sound of almost *shewa* quantity (cf. 22, 23, and for similar sounds in closed syllables 27). This change also occurs in stressed syllables; see 28.

26 ⟨e⟩ = *ṣere*. The statistics given in appendix C, and schematized in paragraph 21, are taken from mss. of class 1, the only texts which maintain a consistent distinction in use between ⟨e⟩ and ⟨e′⟩. The number of examples is, however, too small to provide a trustworthy pattern. If the information of mss. from classes 2 and 3 is included, it is found that the greatest number of examples of this change (111) is found in open, unstressed syllables.[59] On this basis this change is included as an example of pattern 2. The next largest group of examples (88) occurs in closed, stressed final syllables.[60] It is possible that these should be connected with the change described in 29 below, where *ṣere* in closed, stressed final syllables is replaced by an 'a' sign. ⟨e⟩ = *ṣere* also occurs in open, stressed syllables, both final (36 times) and medial (38 times). The very large number of examples of this change in all positions is undoubtedly due to the fact that ⟨e′⟩, the sign expected where bA has *ṣere*, is much less common than ⟨e⟩ in classes 2 and 3 (see appendix B).

27 *Pattern 3* Changes occurring in closed, unstressed syllables.

57 Examples are: ותבאו TS 12:197, Jer. 2:7; שבעתיים Bod. Heb. d55 f. 12v25.

58 Examples are: מיקים Bod. Heb. d63 f. 82r24 (Isa. 44:26), באיבה Ant. 222, 1r17.

59 E.g. שארית TS NS 249:3, Ps. 76:11; המירו TS H16:10, r26 (15:19).

60 E.g. תדבר TS 20:53+, Ps. 37:30; בוחן Bod. Heb. d63 f. 98v17.

	Medial	Final
⟨a′⟩ = *segol*	x	x
⟨i⟩ = *segol*	x	–
⟨a′⟩ = *ḥireq*	x	–
⟨e⟩ = *ḥireq*	xx	–

This pattern shows nothing more than uncertainty as to the quality of vowels in closed, unstressed syllables. Such uncertainty appears even in bA.[61] It is common in Origen's transliterations.[62] The confusion exhibited by Pal. in this situation is really remarkably small. The change ⟨i⟩ = *segol* occurs in six cases in unstressed syllables before laryngeals, as well as in six simple unstressed syllables. These cases could represent the same sort of confusion. They may, however, represent the culmination of an 'a → i' change, since all occur in situations in which such a change has taken place in forms with no laryngeals.[63] Of the other changes, ⟨e⟩ = *ḥireq* occurring in stressed syllables has already been discussed in paragraph 20. It might be correct to include other changes which occur in closed, unstressed syllables under pattern 3.[64]

28 *Pattern 4* Changes occurring in stressed syllables.

	Closed	Open final
⟨u⟩ = *ḥolem*	x	x
⟨a′⟩ = *qameṣ*	xx	x
⟨e′⟩ = *segol*	x	–
⟨i⟩ = *ṣere*	x	x

61 For example, the original 'i' vowel of *qotel* form nouns can be represented by *pataḥ*, *segol*, or *ḥireq* (see Gesenius-Kautzsch, 1910, no. 93qq), and, for *pataḥ*, see forms such as *'oyabtiy*, Mica 7:8, 10.

62 See the figures for the use of *alpha*, *epsilon*, and *iota* where bA has *pataḥ*, *segol*, or *ḥireq* in a closed, unstressed syllable in Brønno, 1943, and his remarks on pp. 454–5.

63 Five occur in *nif'al* forms, e.g. נחשק Bod. Heb. d41 f. 15v2 (43:3); also *ibid.* f. 12r3, 14r31; Ant. 369, p. 16, l. 4; Ant. 912, p. 26, l. 10. The remaining case is ת(הגה) Bod. Heb. e30 f. 48–9+, Isa. 59:3. Such forms occur more commonly in Bab. (see Kahle, 1913, and Porath, 1938). While ben David, 1958 (p. 490), is no doubt right in interpreting such similarities as showing a relationship between the two dialects (i.e., they developed along parallel lines) this fact has no significance for their dates relative to the bA dialect (see paragraph 34). In this particular case, presuming the original vowel of the *nif'al* prefix was 'a,' the statement that the bA *segol* was 'later' than (resulted from development subsequent to) the 'i' of Bab. and Pal. would have to assume a rather complex series of changes for the vowel.

64 ⟨i⟩ = *pataḥ* does also occur (e.g. כרמי' Bod. Heb. d41 f. 15v22, Bar's line 29) but has not been listed because it is rare, and the ⟨i⟩ sign can be explained (often with much probability) as a broken ⟨a⟩.

This pattern probably also indicates confusion. With the exception of ⟨e′⟩ = *segol*, all these changes are listed under pattern 2 (paragraph 21) as occurring in open, unstressed syllables because of weakening of the syllable stress. The reverse of these changes is listed under pattern 1 (paragraph 16), and interpreted as resulting from the effects of primary stress, or of loss of syllable closure under secondary stress. The changes listed under this pattern are assumed to result from confusion caused by the changes in these other two situations. In most cases, the changes listed here occur much more commonly in open, unstressed syllables. The change ⟨a′⟩ = *qameṣ* is evidently a special case. The information given here is taken only from mss. of classes 1, 2, 4, and 6. The frequency of this change in final, stressed syllables is probably due to the influence of the vocalization systems used in classes 3, 5, and 7, where ⟨a⟩ and ⟨a′⟩ are often used interchangeably.[65] The information on ⟨e′⟩ = *segol* given above is taken from mss. of class 1 only. If the information from mss. of classes 2 and 3 is included, this change is found to occur frequently in stressed syllables, closed (12 cases), open final (23 cases), and open non-final (27 cases). The change in the latter two situations might represent a stress-induced quality change of the type described under pattern 1 (paragraph 16). Since, however, it does not occur with any frequency in unstressed syllables before laryngeals or doubled consonants, this change, in all its occurrences in stressed syllables, has been set down to the effects of confusion, as the other changes listed under pattern 4. The same change occurs frequently in closed, final, unstressed syllables (see 30 below).

29 *Pattern 5* Change taking place in closed, stressed final syllables.

⟨a′⟩ = *ṣere*	xx
⟨a⟩ = *ṣere*	x

This pattern shows a special case involving a single situation, and, without doubt, a single sound change. In bA this change would be represented as *ṣere* → *pataḥ*. It represents the culmination of a change 'i → a'. This change had taken place in the stage of Hebrew

65 In these mss., there is a definite tendency to use ⟨a′⟩ rather than ⟨a⟩ in closed, stressed final syllables. Cf. the figures for the 3ms. and 1cs. pronominal suffixes given in paragraph 9. ⟨a⟩ is most commonly used in open, unstressed syllables; thus in TS 12:195+196, ⟨a⟩ is used 171 times in unstressed, and only 56 in stressed syllables. The 2ms. pronoun ⟨-ka⟩ makes up 36 of the latter cases. TS 20:53+ is unique in showing the opposite tendency. In TS 20:54, ⟨a⟩ is used 24 times in stressed, and 19 in unstressed syllables, 17 of the latter cases being word final.

recorded by bA in non-final syllables (Philippi's law) and in some final syllables.[66] In Pal., the change has taken place in the same situations as in bA, and is spreading rapidly to all final syllables. This can cause surprise only to those who think of the Hebrew recorded in bA as an artificially reconstructed dialect which had been maintained for centuries in a completely foreign environment with no possibility of normal development. Such a view is untenable (see note 88). The completion of the change known as 'Philippi's law' was recent when bA was recorded, since this change is not complete in the language transcribed by Origen.[67] Since change must have been in progress so recently before bA was recorded, it is not surprising that it should continue after that time in new situations similar to those in which it had already occurred. That this change did continue is shown in Pal.[68]

30 *Pattern 6* Change taking place in closed, unstressed final syllables.

⟨e′⟩ = *segol* xx

This pattern also shows a special case involving a single situation. The change occurs a total of 53 times in closed, unstressed final syllables, mostly in 'segolate' forms as described in paragraphs 10 and 11, but also elsewhere.[69] It is assumed that a change of quality is involved, since the use of ⟨e′⟩ in this position in segolate forms is

66 See Bauer-Leander (1922), no. 14z, a′, to which can be added (against his no. 45f) the *pi'al* forms found in bA. *Pi'al* forms are common in Bab. (as in Pal.), and are undoubtedly there (as in Pal.) symptomatic of the change of 'i' to 'a' which has taken place in final, stressed syllables in many other forms. E.g. לבֿ and similar forms listed by Kahle, 1913, p. 196, and Porath, 1938, p. 97; *nif'al* imperfects, Kahle, 1913, p. 194, and Porath, 1938, pp. 56f.; *qal* participle, Kahle, 1913, p. 188, and Porath, 1938, pp. 44f. The Bab. sign used in these situations is ע, which represents an 'a' sound (see note 50). The replacement of an original short 'i' vowel by an 'a' vowel in closed, stressed final syllables undoubtedly shows that the Bab. dialect (as the Pal.) has – in this feature at least – developed further than bA, and is therefore 'later.'

67 See Brønno, 1943, p. 448.

68 Examples are: ויפרש J.T.S. ms. 504 f. 2, Jer. 49:22 (must be a variant, *pi'el* for *qal*); חסר TS 20:53+, Ps. 39:11; בירך TS H16:10, v6 (16:1); וניתחנן Bod. Heb. d55 f. 14r7. The same change occurs in a non-final syllable in החלו TS K26:1, Ezra 3:6. With ⟨a⟩, ניתפאר Bod. Heb. d55 f. 14r2; מלמלל Ant. 912, p. 27, l. 11; אדרש TS 20:59+, Ezek. 14:3.

69 E.g. באלהיהם TS 12:195+, Ps. 69:26; תן־ J.T.S. ms. 594, Eccles. 11:2. Such forms as אל TS H16:6, 1r2 (1:2), and את *ibid.* 2v3, 5, 6 (4:6, 8, 9), all of which occur in biblical quotations, should probably also be included here.

dependent on the quality of the preceding vowel (see paragraph 11). If this is the case, the instances in which this change takes place in open syllables after 'a' or 'o' vowels should no doubt be included under this pattern.[70] However, it is impossible to say what vowel qualities would be involved in this change.[71] There is, moreover, some possibility that a change of quantity was involved.[72] Further information is needed before a definite decision can be reached.

The relationship of the Palestinian dialect to that of bA

31 The interchanges of vowel signs just described constitute one of the three major groups of differences between Pal. and bA. No other interchanges occur in significant numbers. Of those described, those showing patterns 1 and 5 appear definitely to show that changes which were in progress in the stage of the language recorded by bA have progressed further in Pal. Changes showing pattern 2 appear to have started from the situation found in bA. The change in pattern 6 is difficult to evaluate, but cannot, I think, be held to represent a stage of the language prior to that recorded

70 This occurs in both stressed syllables (see paragraph 11) and unstressed syllables (e.g. וארחצך TS 20:59, Ezek. 16:9; ואעדך *ibid.*, Ezek. 16:11).

71 There is some possibility that the sound represented by ⟨e′⟩ was close to that represented by ⟨a′⟩. ⟨e′⟩ is often used where bA has *ḥaṭef pataḥ*. Compare also such forms as נעשקה TS 13H2:10, 2v23 (and 24) with נֶעֱצבו Bod. Heb. d55 f. 10v23. However, such usage is common only in mss. in which ⟨e′⟩ is commonly used where bA has *shewa*, and the reasons for considering that the sound represented by ⟨e⟩ was close to an 'a' sound are equally strong.

72 Bod. ms. Heb. c20 f. 25–28 (described in Díez-Macho, 1963, as ms. 31) shows a pointing using *pataḥ* and *ṣere* for all 'a' and 'e' vowels (i.e. comparable to my classes 9–11). 'Segolate' nouns in this ms. usually have *shewa* in the final syllable (e.g. מֵלְךְ, כֵּתְר, in all over 20 times). The *shewa* sign has a much wider use in this ms. than in bA, but probably does represent a '*shewa* vowel' (as ⟨e′⟩ in classes 4 and 5). Contrasting forms are הַאֵרֵץ f. 26v9, נֵצַח 27v16, אֵרֵץ 28v14. This ms. undoubtedly represents a Palestinian tradition of pronunciation (see paragraph 40). The information it gives may be true of the Palestinian dialect in general. In Origen's transliterations vowel signs are not usually written in the final syllable of segolate forms (see Brønno, 1943, pp. 125f.). This cannot indicate that no vowel was used there, as a vowel sign is used in this position in the Septuagint transliterations (see Sperber, 1938, pp. 181f., 185f.), but rather must indicate that the vowel concerned was of *shewa* quantity, since '*shewa* vowels' are usually not indicated in these transliterations, particularly in positions where there could be no doubt of their occurrence. Consequently there is good reason to suppose that ⟨e′⟩ often indicated a vowel of light quantity (cf. also the examples in note 71). However, the supposition that this was always so would conflict with (i) the fact of the free interchange of ⟨e⟩ and ⟨e′⟩ in some situations in the same mss. from which the above facts are drawn (see the figures for the *qal* participle in paragraph 12), and (ii) the use of ⟨e⟩ and ⟨e′⟩ in mss. of class 1 (see paragraph 3).

by bA.[73] Patterns 3 and 4, if they result from confusion, cannot be said to give any indication of development in relation to bA. The information given in paragraphs 16–30, then, strongly suggests that the dialect represented by Pal. was not closer than that of bA to their common origin, but that it had developed further, and was, therefore, in this sense, a 'later' form of the language.

32 The other two typical differences of Pal. from bA are the use of ⟨o⟩ where bA has *qameṣ ḥaṭuf*, and the 'indiscriminate' use (in some mss.) of the 'a' and 'e' signs. The former usage again shows that bA preserves an older pronunciation than Pal. According to the commonly held theory, *qameṣ ḥaṭuf* represents an original 'u' vowel. This 'u' sound is in the process of changing to an 'o' vowel in bA. It is still written as *u* in some closed, unstressed syllables (*hofʿal* of '*prima nun*' verbs). In most, however, *ɔ* is used (e.g. *qɔdšow*). In open, unstressed syllables *ɔ̆* is usually used (*qɔ̆dɔšiym*), but *o* may occur (*ʾohɔliym*). In open, stressed syllables *o* is used (*qódɛš*). In Pal., ⟨o⟩ is found in the great majority of cases in all these situations, showing the change completed. ⟨a⟩ is, however, regularly used where bA has *ḥaṭef qameṣ*, showing that, in the case of vowels of the very smallest quantity, this final change to 'o' quality has not taken place.[74] This shows, then, that Pal. represents a later, more developed, stage of the language than does bA.

33 The same opinion can be derived from the use of the 'a' and 'e' signs in Pal. As was noted above, two 'e' vowels are distinguished by Origen's transliterations. Two 'e' vowels are distinguished in bA. At what period between the two can the situation represented by most Pal. mss., where only one 'e' sign is used, or two are only partially distinguished, have occurred? The answer seems inevitably to be that the situation here was not part of the development from the language recorded by Origen to that of bA. The distinction between two 'e' signs is partial or non-existent in most Palestinian mss. because the distinction between the sounds they represented, although still clear in the stage of the language recorded by bA, was being, or had been, lost in the stage of the language

73 It cannot be argued that ⟨e′⟩ in Pal. ⟨mele′k⟩ represents a lighter vowel than the *segol* in bA *mélɛk*, and therefore an earlier form (as being closer to the presumed original absence of vowel in this position) since bA does not distinguish vowel quantity except in open, unstressed syllables.

74 On the use of ⟨o⟩ in this position see § II.14 and note 135. The use of ⟨a⟩ and ⟨a′⟩ where bA has *qameṣ ḥaṭuf* and of ⟨a′⟩ where bA has *ḥaṭef qameṣ* derives (except probably in class 1) from the influences causing deviation from bA forms (see paragraph 4(iv)).

represented by Pal. A definite trend can be seen in some cases of the use of the 'e' vowels. For example in bA there is a definite tendency to spell nouns of original **qitl* formation *qḗtɛl*, rather than the more characteristic *qétɛl*. In Pal., these nouns are normally written with ⟨e⟩ in the first syllable, as are the original **qatl* types (see paragraph 10 and note 28). This shows that the process of the assimilation of the two types, which has already begun in bA, is completed in Pal., which therefore represents a later form of the language than does bA. The same conclusion can be derived from the use of the 'a' vowels, although the information from the Pal. mss. taken as a whole suggests that the loss of distinction between two 'a' vowels was more recent, and in most areas not so complete, as was the case with the 'e' vowels.

34 All the information given above, then, in so far as it can be said to give any indication at all, shows that the dialect represented by Pal. had developed further from their common origin than had that of bA, and was therefore a 'later' form of the language. Pal. did, of course, retain some forms less developed than those to be found in bA, but such forms are rare and isolated.[75] Taken all in all, Pal. represents a later form of Hebrew than does bA. The common view that the dialect of Pal. is earlier than that of bA appears to be based on a series of assumptions originating with Kahle, and not on any argument. The closest approach to a serious attempt to establish the position of the Palestinian dialect in the history of the language is that of ben David (1958). In the first part of his article, ben David expresses a conclusion similar to that given above, but reached on rather different grounds. He states in substance that Pal. indicated the same pronunciation as bA, but used different signs to do so. Mss. which use seven signs according to the bA system are early, while those which show confusion are late.[76]

75 For instance, לֹּאָרֶץ (TS H7:7, v17) could be taken this way, but not ולֹעֶרֶב (TS K26:1, Ezra 3:3, bA *wəlɔʿɔrɛb*) and similar forms, which testify to the characteristic Pal. use of contextual forms in 'pausal' position. (I have no statistics on this feature of Palestinian Hebrew, but my observations suggest that the (archaic?) 'pausal' forms are frequently not used in Pal.)

76 He does not state specifically that they represent a pronunciation later than that of bA, but this is implicit in his argument: Pal. represents substantially the same dialect as bA (p. 483b). Confusion of ⟨a⟩ and ⟨a′⟩ or ⟨e⟩ and ⟨e′⟩ is due to ignorance and is therefore not early (p. 484a; by this argument, it must in fact be later than the 'original' stage which is shown in bA and related Pal. texts). The bA distinction of *pataḥ* and *qameṣ* reflects the pronunciation of the *naqdanim*, but 'only those who used the "non-Masoretic" (i.e. Palestinian) pronunciation confused it (the distinction) and did not know how to use the two signs' (p. 484b; clearly he is suggesting that the distinction was not present in their pronunciation, which is therefore, by his argument, later than that of bA).

Further on in the same article, however, he states that the dialect represented by Pal. is, in fact, earlier than that of bA (p. 485). He does not make clear why he does this, or how he reconciles this attitude with his first, but presumably the reason is the similarities between Pal. and Bab. noted in his section 12, since in his chronological arrangement (p. 485) he places the dialect of Bab. much earlier than that of bA. This is, of course, a gross oversimplification.[77] As far as our information goes, all three dialects were in use contemporaneously. Bab. does contain some factors which appear to show that the dialect it represents had developed less far from a common original, in some respects, than that of bA. It also contains some phenomena, however, which would appear to indicate the reverse.[78] It is ludicrous to suppose that if different dialects developed from a common original under different influences (as must have been the case with the Babylonian dialect and those of Palestine) one must of necessity be a uniformly earlier stage of the language than the other. Consequently agreements between Bab. and Pal. against bA cannot be held to be 'early' elements of the language just because Bab. is involved, but must be judged by some other criterion. It is not easy to judge all ben David's examples. In some cases he may be right in his claim that they represent features of the languages less developed than the corresponding features in bA. However, this is not the case with the majority, as is argued in the following paragraphs.

35 The first point raised by ben David concerns the pointing of conjunctive *waw*. Where bA points this conjunction as *shureq*, Pal. and Bab. usually point it as *w* followed by a '*shewa* vowel.' The information of Origen's transliterations does not permit a definite conclusion, but suggests that the bA spelling represents the older form.[79] A study of the Palestinian mss. shows that (i) the 'u' form is much more common in biblical mss. than in non-biblical; (ii) this form is used in biblical mss. which show no (other) trace of

77 It is, moreover, in direct contrast to his earlier conclusion, as the features which he notes as similar to Bab. are most common in the mss. most dissimilar to bA (see HTPV, chapter v). Sperber, 1959, p. 77, also relying on a single criterion, concludes that the dialect represented by Pal. is earlier than that of Bab.

78 E.g. the change 'i → a' in stressed syllables has progressed much further in Bab. than in bA (see note 66). The common use of the same sign in **qitl* type as in **qatl* type 'segolate' nouns (see Kahle, 1913, pp. 195f.; Porath, 1938, pp. 100f.) also indicates a development beyond that recorded in bA (see paragraph 33).

79 Origen's transliterations use a vowel sign after *ou* representing conjunctive *waw* only in rare cases. However, the cases in which a vowel sign is used in this position are difficult to explain. See Brønno, 1943, pp. 227f.

bA influence;[80] (iii) in non-biblical mss. the use of this form is confined to mss. of classes 2, 4, and 6, which use the 'a' signs, but not the 'e' signs, as does bA (there is no information from class 1); (iv) in biblical class 3, and non-biblical class 2, the use of the 'u' form is not homogeneous, some mss. using this form, some the *w* + '*shewa* vowel' form, some both.[81] Points (ii) and (iii) indicate that this 'u' form in Palestinian Hebrew is not copied from bA, but rather derives from certain strata of the Palestinian system. Points (i) and (iii) indicate that it derives from the more conservative strata in which the dialect has resisted change (see 38 below). Point (iv) shows that the systems of pointing developed in the less conservative strata sometimes did, and sometimes did not, use this form. Presumably, then, they derived this usage from traditions or mss. which, since these less conservative strata (classes 3, 5, 7, and also 2) are manifestly not related to bA or Bab., must have been indigenous in Palestinian circles. Consequently there are very good reasons for supposing that bA's writing of conjunctive *waw* as *shureq* represents an earlier stage of the language than the other spelling more common in Pal. and Bab., and the Pal. mss. which use ⟨u⟩ here are using an archaic form.

36 The other two major points raised by ben David concern interchanges of vowel signs. He believes the interchange of 'a' and 'e' signs to show, in Pal., the vestiges of an 'a' and 'e' vowel system similar to that of Bab. It should be noted at once that even if such confusion does occur in Pal., it does not per se show that the Palestinian dialect was either closer to Babylonian than, or earlier than that of bA. Such confusion exists in bA; e.g. in the imperfect *qal* of *'sr*, *ḥémat/ḥémɛt*, etc. (see also paragraph 27). Reasons have already been given for thinking that most cases of such interchange have no connection with the Babylonian dialect (see paragraph 19 and note 50), but ben David includes in his examples some of the occasional Pal. uses of ⟨e⟩ or ⟨e'⟩ where bA has *ḥaṭef pataḥ*. I know of 25 cases of the use of ⟨e'⟩ in this position, all in non-biblical mss. All follow laryngeals (cf. paragraph 19). Eighteen cases occur in mss. of classes 4 and 5 where ⟨e'⟩ is used virtually only where bA has *shewa* (see note

80 E.g. TS NS 249:8+ (class 3) and Bod. Heb. d29 f. 17-20 (class 7). These are mss. no. 3 and no. 7 in Dietrich's list of 21 mss. The highest numbers in this list designate the closest mss. to bA.

81 TS 12:195+ (class 3) uses the '*waw* + *shewa* vowel' spelling. This ms. is no. 16 in Dietrich's list (see note 87). Of the four biblical mss. in class 7, two use the 'u' spelling, two give no pointed examples. Bod. ms. Heb. d55 f. 12v–14v (class 2, non-biblical) does not use the 'u' spelling, but it is used in TS H16:6, 7, and Ant. 369, all of the same class. In TS 13H2:11+12 (class 6) both pointings are used.

55). Five more occur in Bodleian ms. Heb. d55 f. 12v–14v (class 2) in which ⟨e′⟩ is also often used where bA has simple *shewa*. These cases presumably indicate nothing more than the use of a 'simple' rather than a 'coloured' sign for a '*shewa* vowel.' The remaining two cases occur in mss. of class 7. In each case ⟨e′⟩ is used only once in the ms. Its use is, therefore, without determinable significance.[82] ⟨e⟩ is used in 21 cases where bA has *ḥaṭef pataḥ*, all but two following laryngeals. Eleven occur in biblical mss., all in mss. in which ⟨e⟩ is commonly used where bA has simple *shewa*. Presumably these cases also show nothing more than the use of a 'simple' instead of a 'coloured' *shewa* sign.[83] If ⟨e⟩ and ⟨e′⟩ in these cases represent '*shewa* vowels,' they do not indicate confusion of 'a' and 'e' sounds, and so no connection with Bab.

37 The last major point raised by ben David is the replacement of ⟨u⟩ by ⟨o⟩. This has already been discussed above (paragraph 17). The other categories which he considers to show connection with the Babylonian dialect are only represented by a few forms, and so are of little significance. Some of these may be genuine examples of the retention of old forms in both dialects. Such a situation would not be surprising (see note 75). They may equally well, however, be cases in which both dialects have developed further than bA from their common original, as is the case where Pal. and Bab. use 'a' signs where bA has *ṣere* in closed, final, stressed syllables (see paragraph 29 and note 66) and other cases discussed above.

38 The uses of vowel signs in which Pal. differs from bA, then, show that bA represents the 'older' form of the language. The Palestinian pointing must reflect a dialect which was more open to foreign influence, and so changed faster, than that of bA. The Palestinian mss. do not give any real indication of the nature of the community for which they were written.[84] They do, however, give at least one clear indication of the type of influence which caused their peculiarities. The only consistent morphological difference between these mss. and bA is the use of the -VC form of the 2ms. pronominal suffix (bA -*ɔk*) instead of the -CV form characteristic

82 Bod. Heb. d63 f. 87r8 and TS H16:1, v19 (30:11). I presume that both signs are due to secondary hands.

83 This usage is common enough in Tiberian mss. of 'non-bA' types (see, e.g., Díez-Macho, 1963*a*, p. 21). In my opinion, a writing such as י(ר)דפ(ך) (TS NS 249:5, Ezek. 35:6) clinches the matter.

84 However, Weinrich's suggestion (1964, pp. 142, 146) that Pal. represents a 'south Israeli' dialect, cut off from Tiberias by the Samaritan community, would appear to have a good deal to recommend it.

of bA (-*kɔ*). The careful study of ben Hayyim has shown that this usage is restricted to the Palestinian non-biblical mss., and is derived from Aramaic.[85] This shows, then, that the Palestinian dialect was, at some point in its earlier history, heavily influenced by Aramaic. The pronunciation used for the biblical texts, however, did not come under this influence, but preserved the older -CV suffix form as did bA (-*kɔ*). It has already been shown that Pal. biblical texts differentiated the two 'a' and the two 'e' signs in more cases, and did so more consistently than did the non-biblical texts.[86] It is also true that biblical texts contain proportionately fewer uses of other vowel signs divergent from those of bA than do non-biblical texts.[87] Biblical texts therefore show, in general, a form of language closer to bA, and therefore (since bA represents the 'older' form of the language) more old fashioned, more carefully preserved, than do the non-biblical texts. The corollary of this is, of course, that bA represents a pronunciation even more carefully preserved than do the Palestinian biblical texts.

The Palestinian dialects

39 The 'Palestinian biblical' pronunciation was used only for formal reading of the biblical text, as is shown by the fact that it is not used in the biblical quotations in the liturgical texts. Throughout these texts another form of pronunciation was used. This was not well preserved. It has been influenced by Aramaic, as is shown by its consistent use of the -VC form of the 2ms. pronominal suffix. The same influence, together with that of the various other languages which had been spoken in Palestine, must have caused the loss of vowel distinctions and the change in vowel quality in the various positions noted.[88] The language of the non-biblical texts,

85 See ben Hayyim, 1954*a*, pp. 27–32, 63. As regards the use of the -CV form suffix in non-biblical texts, a longer list could now be given than that on p. 30, since more texts are known. The observation made there that these forms always follow vowels (other than '*shewa* vowels') or are direct quotations of biblical forms remains true, although such a quotation can appear within a poem.

86 This is true generally. Specific instances are given in paragraphs 8, 10, 11.

87 E.g. ⟨o⟩ = *shureq*: biblical texts, 14 examples; non-biblical, 78 examples; ⟨a'⟩ = *ṣere*: biblical, 4 examples; non-biblical, 27 examples.

88 I have no doubt that the process of linguistic change normal within a living language was a contributory cause. So much material has now been brought to light that it has become very difficult to show a period when the Hebrew language could have been out of use. Processes of morphological change can be seen between the Hebrew of the Old Testament, Qumran, and the early *piyyuṭim*. For instance, the loss of final *he* (and presumably its preceding vowel) in '*lamed-he*' verbs occurs in *waw*-consecutive and jussive forms in biblical Hebrew; in other imperfect forms, apparently at the author's option, in Qumrani Hebrew; and in both perfect

then, represents the informal, colloquial pronunciation of Palestine and adjacent areas. This colloquial pronunciation in Liturgy was very persistent, as has been demonstrated by A. Spanier, who showed that the -VC second person suffix form, and other characteristics of the 'Palestinian' dialect, were used in the prayer-books of various European communities.[89] Similar material is to be found in Yalon's discussion of the pointing of the Mishna,[90] and, indeed, in most other discussions of mediaeval Hebrew pronunciation which I have seen.[91] The fact that such 'Palestinian' features occur in a Mishna ms. believed to have been pointed by Maimonides[92] shows that such pronunciation was not a feature of ignorant and unorthodox communities, but was the normal pronunciation of Hebrew, even among the greatest scholars, and was used in all situations, except for the formal reading of the biblical text.

40 This colloquial dialect was, then, in use over a wide area, both of space and of time. The number of Palestinian mss. known may be considered disproportionately small. However, the mss. of the so-called ben Naftali type represent the same tradition.[93] Mss. of this group can be found with five, six, or seven vowel signs besides *shewa*.[94] They thus parallel the various types of Palestinian mss. They contrast with the Palestinian texts in that they use the *shewa* sign, but this is to be expected since the invention of this sign made the Tiberian system a much more efficient method of recording the language than was Pal. (see § II.9, 15). Apart from this, the pointing of the 'ben Naftali' texts is, in general, consistent with Palestinian

---

and imperfect forms, again at the author's option, in the *piyyuṭim* (see Zunz, 1920, pp. 381f. for examples). No doubt a detailed study would show similar cases of morphological development. This article claims to show that phonological development also took place. At least in the more conservative texts, the pace of this does not seem too great for 'natural' development (i.e. not induced by overwhelming foreign influence).

89 Spanier, 1929. See now also Bét-Aryé, 1965, pp. 93ff.

90 Yalon, 1964.

91 It is rash to generalize on such a complex problem, but it would seem that such gross characteristics as the use of the -VC 2ms. pronoun form, and the confusion of *qameṣ* and *pataḥ* and of *segol* and *ṣere*, must derive ultimately from the Palestinian dialect, as the Babylonian divergences from bA were quite different.

92 Yalon, 1964, pp. 33–4.

93 First suggested, I believe, in Morag, 1959, and most recently elaborated in Díez-Macho, 1963*a*.

94 Examples using only *pataḥ* and *ṣere* (i.e. with two 'a' and 'e' vowels) are Bod. Heb. c20 f. 25–28 (see note 72) and TS E1:95 (mishnaic). Biblical examples are rare, but do exist, e.g. TS NS 42:1. With three 'a' and 'e' vowels: lacking *qameṣ*, TS B6:2 (see Díez-Macho, 1963*a*, pp. 36f.); lacking *segol* (virtually), J.T.S. ms. 503 (ENA 2116) f. 15–16 (see *ibid.*, ms. 4), and numerous non-biblical texts. Many mss. are also found using four 'a' and 'e' vowel signs, but confusing *qameṣ* and *pataḥ* and *segol* and *ṣere* (see the descriptions in Díez-Macho, 1963*a*).

customs.[95] There can, I think, be no doubt that these mss. represent a pronunciation different from that of bA, as do the Pal. texts. Goshen-Gottstein argues that no important difference was involved. His suggestion that the sounds represented by *segol* and *ṣere* were allophones of the same phoneme is certainly debatable,[96] but in any case the point of phonemic status is irrelevant. We have the evidence of Saadya that the two signs represented different sounds,[97] and the evidence of bA that the two signs were not free variants. The 'ben Naftali' texts manifestly use the two signs in a manner different from that of bA, and sometimes use only one sign in place of the two. Consequently 'ben Naftali' texts must have been pronounced differently from those of bA. Their common use of Tiberian signs indicates not their common tradition,[98] but their common recognition of the efficiency of the Tiberian pointing system. No doubt the difference in pronunciation was not considered important by the populace, so long as it did not coincide with sectarian or other local differences. It is equally certain, however, that no grammarian would consider the difference unimportant.[99] Comparatively little work has been done on these 'ben Naftali' type mss., particularly on the non-biblical ones, so judgment on their position must be provisional. However, it seems at present that they

95 See Díez-Macho, 1963*a*, pp. 20f.

96 I presume that this is what is meant by 'the opposition of the graphemes *ṣere versus segol* cannot be said to be phonemic' (*sic*. Goshen-Gottstein, 1963, p. 98, not 65) but I find the note difficult to understand. For an argument that both signs indicate phonemes, see Morag, 1962, p. 22, note 17.

97 See Skoss, 1952, p. 293. Ben Hayyim's opinion that Saadya is discussing Babylonian pronunciation is based on (and probably referred to) one point only. See ben Hayyim, 1953, p. 90, where it is concluded that, when Saadya mentions a method of deciding whether *pataḥ*, *segol*, or *ṣere* is to be used in a word, he refers to Bab., as 'only there are *pataḥ* and *segol* identical.' He could quite as well have Pal. in mind, as most Pal. mss. use only one 'e' sign where bA has *segol* and *ṣere*. Presumably the Ga'on is speaking generally of possible confusions, such as those guarded against by the notes on the spelling of forms of *'kl*, *hlk*, *ḥrb*, etc. in *Diqduqe haṬəʿamim*. In any case the constant mention of *pataḥ* and *segol* as distinct in Saadya's work shows that the study in general deals with the pronunciation of bA. This would, of course, include the description of the position of the vowels in the mouth.

98 As is suggested by their being contrasted to Pal. in Goshen-Gottstein, 1963, p. 112, no. 40. For the view taken here, see also now Morag, 1965, p. 209.

99 I know of no grammarian who supports Goshen-Gottstein's view, or who fails to list *segol* and *ṣere* as representing distinct vowels. The practice of correcting divergent mss. to agree with bA and the trend of 'ben Naftali' mss. towards harmonization with bA (Díez-Macho, 1963*a*, p. 18) also show that such differences were not ignored. As regards the 'a' signs – again if I understand his note 65, p. 98 correctly – Goshen-Gottstein, 1963, foresees the possibility that mss. which did not distinguish two 'a' signs may have been written. Admittedly the distinction between the 'a' signs (and vowels) was more stable than that between the 'e' signs, but mss. which use only one 'a' sign certainly exist (see note 101).

can be taken as mss. representing the Palestinian dialect in Tiberian signs. As such, they show that the Palestinian tradition had a much wider use than would be supposed from the number of mss. with Palestinian pointing.

The development of the Palestinian and ben Asher dialects

41 The following is a tentative outline of the events which produced the situation described above. The earliest evidence of a difference between the colloquial and the formal pronunciations of Hebrew appears in the scrolls of Qumran Cave I.[100] These apparently reproduce the colloquial pronunciation, as would be expected from a consideration of the orthography of many mss. The same colloquial pronunciation appears in the classical transliterations.[101] It is certain, however, that the colloquial and the formal dialects were developing side by side, as Origen's transliterations show some processes to be in progress which are completed in the bA dialect.[102] However, the biblical or formal pronunciation was the more conservative, although probably not consciously so at first. The difference between biblical and mishnaic Hebrew evidently only became a subject of rabbinic comment at the end of the third century A.D.[103] It is unlikely that before this time, or even for some time after, any particular value was attached to an exact formal pronunciation of vowel sounds.[104] This would parallel the state of affairs at Qumran in the case of the text. No value appears to have been attached to exactitude of spelling, or even of wording. The tradition which became M.T. was in existence, but, as far as

100 It is dated here on the basis of the *-k* and *-kh* forms of the 2ms. pronominal suffix which appear to be free variants at that time. Other evidence could be adduced, but the phonological interpretation of Qumrani orthography is not sufficiently certain to make this of value. It is possibly to be connected with the rise of 'mishnaic Hebrew,' in which case it can perhaps be set earlier (see Segal, 1927, p. 14).

101 This is also predicated mainly on the basis of the form of the 2ms. pronominal suffix, but other phenomena in Origen probably indicate the same; e.g. his use of *omicron* where bA has *qameṣ ḥaṭuf* (see paragraph 32). That Origen's pronunciation should be 'colloquial' is not surprising. His transliteration was surely intended to make clear the grammatical forms in the text, and so served the same purpose as did the later pointing systems. He would not have been interested in the formal ceremonial pronunciation, or even in showing the pronunciation very exactly, hence he did not represent certain insignificant vowels – e.g. in the second syllable of 'segolate' nouns (see note 72).

102 E.g. 'Philippi's law' (see paragraph 29), the change in colour of the vowel of the first syllable of 'segolate' nouns of original **qatl* form from 'a' to 'e,' etc.

103 See Segal, 1927, p. 3.

104 Thus in *Berakhoth* 2:3, opinion on the necessity of clear pronunciation of consonants is divided. In the talmudic comment on this point, the necessity

we can tell, did not approach exclusiveness in use until much later.[105] In the same way, the dialect from which the bA pronunciation sprang was undoubtedly in use at an early date, but it does not seem to have been widely regarded as the best pronunciation for ceremonial reading until after the production of the bA pointing system.

42 At some point between the transliterations of Origen and the first of our Palestinian mss., the distinction between the two 'a' vowels and between the two 'e' vowels began to disappear in the colloquial dialect. Apparently the distinction between the two 'e' vowels was lost first, as it is lacking in more mss.[106] These and other changes which took place in the colloquial dialect did not significantly affect the formal pronunciation which became the bA dialect. By this time the formal dialect was probably being consciously preserved by the group of scholars who used it, so that it did not undergo any of the changes current in colloquial speech. The 'Palestinian' scholars did not take equal care with the preservation of their ceremonial pronunciation so that, although it did retain some ancient features, it was not outstandingly conservative compared to the colloquial pronunciation, except in its use of the -CV form of the second person pronominal suffix. The vowel system of their formal pronunciation therefore followed the same line of development as did their colloquial speech, but more slowly.[107] It presumably represents a stage of the language between that of the non-biblical texts and that of bA.[108]

---

of care where confusion of consonants might produce an irreverent meaning is noted. After this the Jerusalem Talmud notes that Jews from certain areas are not allowed to undertake the ceremonial reading of the biblical text because of their incorrect pronunciation of certain consonants. There is no indication of concern for the pronunciation of vowels until the masoretic literature.

105 I see no reason to assume that Qumran differed much in this respect from the average Jewish community of this time. On this see now Talmon, 1964, especially pp. 97f.

106 This fact may show a significant connection with the Samaritan pointing system, which uses one 'e' and two 'a' signs. However, if ben Hayyim, 1954*b*, is right in his view of the origin of the second Samaritan 'a' vowel, the system can have no direct connection with Pal. (see pp. 523f.).

107 An indication of this slowness, and of the general tendency to conservatism in these texts, is that although many confuse the two 'a' signs, no Palestinian biblical text, at least of any extent, uses only one 'a' sign, while a number of non-biblical ones do. (See paragraph 3. Dietrich, 1968, in the chart on p. 88*, does list texts as showing only one 'a' sign, but the amount of pointed material they contain is too small to permit the assumption that the original text did not use two.)

108 For distinction between the pronunciation of biblical and non-biblical texts in other communities, see Morag, 1963, p. 14. The various classes of Pal.

43 We do not know who these 'Palestinians' were. As has been shown (paragraph 39) their colloquial pronunciation can be ascribed neither to unorthodox nor to ignorant elements. They even used, in their study of the biblical text, some of the same masoretic material as did the 'Tiberians.'[109] Their biblical texts do contain some variants from that of ben Asher, but these are not of great importance.[110] No doubt such texts stem from a group which could be considered lax and unorthodox only by the most conservative.[111] They must have produced their pointing system before, or at any rate in ignorance of the perfection of, that of ben Asher.[112] To judge from the contents of the Geniza, the acceptance of the bA pointing system, and also the pronunciation which it enshrined, was quick in most areas. It is easy to see why the pointing system was accepted: it was more efficient than Pal. for the recording of the Hebrew pronunciation. As such it was used by the producers of the 'ben Naftali' mss. to reproduce the Pal. tradition. The bA pronunciation itself was probably accepted quickly because it was recognizably superior. This superiority no doubt lay partly in the integrity of those who had preserved the pronunciation, and in the obvious validity of their claim to be the bearers of authoritative tradition. In my opinion, however, the superiority lay also in the fact that the bA pronunciation preserved a number of features which were only partially preserved in the Palestinian biblical pronunciation, or perhaps only faintly remembered by its scholars.

---

pointing in both biblical and non-biblical texts show various degrees of conservatism. They fall into two main groups, one of which is 'conservative,' using the 'a' signs much as does bA, while the second group confuses them. Compare the characteristics of classes 4 and 6 with classes 5 and 7 as given in paragraph 3.

109 See, e.g., Weil, 1962, p. 70.

110 See, e.g., Kahle, 1930, p. 37*, and Dietrich, 1968, pp. 71ff. On those pages Dietrich studies the variants in the texts which he publishes, compares them with the collected variants to the ben Asher text, and concludes that they can be divided into four groups, each of which has a 'vulgarizing' tendency (p. 105). This is tantamount to saying of the textual tradition what this article claims for the pronunciation: that the Palestinian was less closely guarded from change than was that of ben Asher.

111 Among other indications it should be noted that much of their liturgical poetry was by well-known *payyeṭanim*, and much of it appears in Italian and Ashkenazic prayer-books.

112 Otherwise they would have used a sign corresponding to bA *shewa*, as is done in the Palestinian texts of the 'ben Naftali' type. An approach to this is made (possibly under bA influence) in some Pal. texts, but a sign with equivalent function was never developed. See § 11 of this article.

II 'SHEWA VOWELS' IN PALESTINIAN HEBREW

1. In his *Materials for a Non-Masoretic Hebrew Grammar*, vol. III (Helsinki, 1964), pp. 13–14, A. Murtonen attacks the view expressed by ben David and other scholars that Palestinian Hebrew used *shewa* much as did bA. One problem raised is that of terminology. The term '*shewa*' will be used here to indicate the Tiberian sign only. A second problem, the extent to which it is correct to search for Tiberian categories in other dialects, is surely resolved by the fact that Palestinian mss. do not provide sufficient homogeneous material for a complete linguistic description of the language. Comparison is, therefore, the only possible method of procedure. With these questions settled thus, it is hoped here to establish, at least in a preliminary way, the nature of the vowels used in Palestinian Hebrew where bA uses *shewa*, and so to settle some of the questions raised by Murtonen's arguments in the above-mentioned book.

2 Since bA is to be used as a standard of comparison, the first requirement is a statement of the value of bA *shewa* as understood here. Murtonen appears to understand that when ben David uses *shewa* as the name of a sound, he means a vowel of a particular quality. Whether or not this is true of ben David, it is surely not true of the early Hebrew grammarians. Their characteristic description of 'seven vowels and *shewa*' clearly attests the unique value of the *shewa* sign. This is inexplicable if *shewa* indicates merely a short vowel of a particular quality. The fact is, of course, that, as these same grammarians point out, *shewa* could indicate a vowel of any quality, depending on its situation.[113] The rules for the pronunciation of the vowels indicated by *shewa* vary somewhat among the grammars. It is one of the merits of the Tiberian system that it cut through the various local differences, and used a single sign to denote any '*shewa* vowel,' i.e. any vowel sound in an open, unstressed (i.e. tertiary stressed, see note 46) syllable. Rules were easily compiled to indicate the correct quality of '*shewa* vowel' in

113 See the examples in 11–13 below. Garbell, 1959, pp. 153–4, argues that *shewa* is treated differently from the seven 'full vowels' because it never represents a vowel phoneme. This is questionable (see, e.g., Morag, 1962, p. 23), but even if it were true this argument would stand, since – as Garbell agrees – vowels were undoubtedly produced where bA writes *shewa*. The pronunciation of these vowels was clearly a matter of concern to the grammarians and *naqdanim*, whether they were phonemic or not.

any special situation.[114] Otherwise the vowel produced was probably a fairly central, neutral one, which the grammarians liken to *pataḥ* or *segol*. The exact realization no doubt varied from place to place.

3 In some cases the quality of a '*shewa* vowel' could not be determined by context, but it was necessary that a particular quality be used, such as after a laryngeal. Here the quality was indicated by the placing of one of the 'quality signs' (a 'full vowel' sign) beside the *shewa*. Where it indicates a vowel, then, *shewa* indicates vowel *quantity* and so is distinct from the other Tiberian vowel signs, all of which indicate quality.[115] It seems futile to speculate on the reason for the use of the same sign where no vowel was pronounced. I would suggest, however, that one reason was the identical intention of avoiding involvement in local differences. No doubt then, as is the case in modern Hebrew today, some pronounced a '*shewa* vowel' where others did not. The same problem is implicit in the term '*shewa* medium.' This phenomenon, if it did exist in speech, must have occurred in other positions as well as before the '*begad kefat*' consonants, and must, then, have presented a considerable problem to the vocalizer. bA, then, distinguished clearly the seven vowel qualities where this was easily done: in syllables under primary or secondary stress ('tone' and 'pretonic' syllables). In other positions, a sign neutral as to quality was used, and its interpretation left to rule of thumb and local custom, except in the special case of the 'composite *shewa*.'

4 The Palestinian system never developed a sign equivalent to bA *shewa*. The four 'a' and 'e' signs are all used where bA uses *shewa*, as is ⟨i⟩ less commonly, and ⟨o⟩ and ⟨u⟩ rarely. Some mss. did, however, come very near the bA development. Unfortunately the ms. in which this is most nearly achieved is still unpublished. This is the Cambridge ms. TS NS 249:14+.[116] In this ms., ⟨a'⟩ is used 56 times where bA uses *shewa*. Elsewhere it corresponds to *ḥaṭef pataḥ* 7 times, *pataḥ* 14 times. As a rule, and of course much more frequently, ⟨a⟩ is used where bA uses both *qameṣ* and *pataḥ*, and also five times corresponding to *ḥaṭef pataḥ*. It seems obvious that in

114 For references to the grammarians, see notes 131, 134. The difficulty is to know how the *shewa* was pronounced normally, not in the special cases. See Levy, 1936, p. 41.

115 This point is made, from a different point of view, in Morag, 1962, p. 27.

116 The mss. referred to in this article are listed, with bibliography, in appendix A.

this ms. ⟨a′⟩ was used almost solely to indicate '*shewa* vowels.'[117] It is even possible that some of the other uses of ⟨a′⟩ derive from a second hand.[118]

5 Similar special use of a vowel sign is found in mss. of classes 4 and 5 (see § 1.3) which use ⟨e′⟩ almost solely where bA uses *shewa*. For example in TS H16:4, ⟨e′⟩ is used 14 times where bA would use *shewa*. In its only other use it corresponds to bA *qameṣ* (r10), but here also it probably represents a '*shewa* vowel' (see § 1. 23). ⟨i⟩ is used 4 times where bA would have *shewa* before *yod*, a characteristic Palestinian usage. The only other sign corresponding to bA *shewa* is ⟨a′⟩ (twice, v9). This is the most complete case of such specialization that I know of. Many mss. use ⟨e′⟩ in this way, but it is never the only, and not always the most common, sign used where bA would use *shewa*.

6 These two instances show the beginning, in Palestinian circles, of the specialization of one sign for use where bA uses *shewa*, and therefore presumably to indicate '*shewa* vowels.' A different type of specialization is found in Palestinian mss. of class 1, in which the use of vowel signs is most similar to that of bA. Examples are Bod. ms. Heb. e30 f. 48–9+ and TS H16:10. In mss. of this type ⟨e⟩ is regularly used where bA uses *segol*. It is also used almost exclusively where bA uses *shewa*, but it is not used elsewhere. Here, then, we have a single sign used in what, in bA, are two different sets of grammatical positions. The other Pal. signs, in mss. of this class, each correspond to a single bA sign. It cannot be doubted that, in these mss. where ⟨e⟩ corresponds to bA *shewa*, it indicates a '*shewa* vowel.'

7 A further argument for the existence of '*shewa* vowels' in Palestinian Hebrew is the fact that some mss. fail almost entirely to represent them.[119] An 'argument from silence' is not normally im-

117 Other signs correspond to bA *shewa* a total of 10 times in this ms. All but four of these cases represent characteristic Palestinian differences from bA (such as the use of ⟨i⟩ where bA has *shewa* before *yod*).

118 More than one hand has certainly worked on this ms. (see IITPV 11.8). It is, however, in most cases difficult to distinguish the additions from the original pointing.

119 See Morag, 1962, p. 34, but he is wrong in referring to either of the mss. published in Kahle, 1927, as a ms. of this type. In TS H16:3 (the '*24 Priesterordnungen*' ms.), ⟨a′⟩ is commonly used where bA would have *shewa*. The Levias Yannai ms. is of the type described in paragraph 5. In the Hebrew portions of the various fragments which form part of this ms. (see appendix A under H.U.C. ms. 1001) ⟨e′⟩ is used 40 times where bA would use *shewa*. Other signs are used a total of 25 times.

pressive, but it is surely not mere coincidence that, for instance, TS H16:6 and Bodleian ms. Heb. d63 f. 98, neither of which is sparing in its use of vowel signs, show respectively six and three signs only, in all of the positions where bA would use *shewa*.[120] Among the unpublished Palestinian mss., there are some which never use a vowel sign where bA would use *shewa*.[121]

8 The instances given show that the Palestinians did have vowels where bA uses *shewa*. Paragraphs 4–7 describe four different types of ms. in which the vowels occurring where bA uses *shewa* are treated uniformly in four different ways. This use of different signs in different groups of mss. would surely not be possible if the vowels represented were either *shewa* quantity vowels of a single quality, or vowels of varying qualities and of 'full vowel' quantity. It must therefore be concluded that they were '*shewa* vowels' as defined in paragraph 2.

9 Such uniform treatment is, however, relatively rare. Most mss. use ⟨a′⟩ and ⟨e⟩ or ⟨e′⟩, apparently indiscriminately, where bA uses *shewa*. However, the use of 'a' and 'e' vowels is exactly what we should expect from the statements of the early grammarians on the pronunciation of *shewa*. The very fact of indiscriminate use should show that this was not a case of representing full vowels of recognized quality, but '*shewa* vowels.'[122] There is, therefore, no reason to doubt that in most cases where bA has vocal *shewa*, the Palestinians had the same type of vowel, i.e. a '*shewa* vowel' as defined in paragraph 2. However, the Palestinians never achieved the representa-

120 Vowel signs occur in these mss. where bA has a composite *shewa* only five times, all in TS H16:6, all corresponding to *ḥaṭef pataḥ*.

121 This is typical in class 6. Most mss. of this class are sparsely vocalized. TS H2:30, however, is an example which never uses vowel signs where bA would have *shewa*, but which has otherwise fairly heavy vocalization. It uses about as many vowel signs as TS H16:10, which has some 14 signs corresponding to bA *shewa*.

122 Against this it might be argued that the use of the two 'a' and of the two 'e' vowels shows little uniformity in many mss. However, this is not so true as is generally maintained (see § 1.8–12). As regards '*shewa* vowels,' in TS 13H2:10 the use of the two 'a' vowels is almost identical with the use of *qameṣ* and *pataḥ* in bA. However, where bA uses *shewa*, the following occur: ⟨e′⟩ 17 times, ⟨a′⟩ 7 times, ⟨i⟩ 4 times, ⟨a⟩ twice, ⟨e⟩ once. Consequently, it cannot be maintained that there is a connection between the plurality of signs corresponding to bA *shewa* and the other common confusion. Moreover, while the interchange of ⟨a⟩ with ⟨a′⟩, and of ⟨e⟩ with ⟨e′⟩, is common, that of 'a' signs with 'e' signs is rare, and takes place in a few specific situations (see § 1.19, 23, 27, 29, 36). The fact that this is not true of the signs corresponding to bA *shewa* shows again that a different type of vowel is here indicated. Finally, it is possible that further study will show more order and method in the common Palestinian use of 'a' and 'e' signs for *shewa* vowels than is at present visible.

tion of such vowels by a sign which was not, in normal use, tied to a specific vowel quality. It was this achievement which made the position of *shewa* in the Tiberian and Babylonian systems so very much clearer. When compared to them, the Palestinian transcription of *shewa* vowels can only be described as experimental.

10 However, this 'experimental quality' should not be taken as an indication that 'true' Palestinian Hebrew did not have '*shewa* vowels,' and, in mss. in which they are clearly indicated, copied them from the Tiberians. It must be remembered that we are comparing bA, the most polished product of the Tiberian masoretic schools, with a pointing of which there is no recognizable standard form, but 10 or so different systems. It is not to be expected that Palestinian pointing should be as consistent as bA. Furthermore some mss. do reach a remarkable level of consistency and detail in the representation of the quality of '*shewa* vowels.' This detail in representation of quality gives such mss. a most peculiar appearance to one habituated to bA. It must be remembered, however, that this is largely due to the fact that bA did not need such detail, having a *shewa* sign which did not indicate a particular vowel quality.

11 The best example of such detail in the representation of '*shewa* vowel' quality is Bodleian ms. Heb. d55 f. 12v–14v.[123] In this ms., ⟨e⟩ is used to indicate most '*shewa* vowels.'[124] Less commonly a special sign $\preceq$ is used.[125] ⟨o⟩ is used in three cases where bA would have *shewa* before *'alef* followed by *ḥolem*.[126] ⟨i⟩ is used

123 The second part of Murtonen, 1958, ms. a. Murtonen (p. 29) recognizes some differences between the parts, but does not consider them important. The use of signs for '*shewa* vowels' (among other things) is, however, completely different in the two parts, as is shown below. Consequently only folios 12v–14v are considered here. In fols. 4r–12r (and in TS H16:9, which forms part of the same ms.) the signs used where bA uses *shewa* are: ⟨a′⟩ some 148 times, ⟨e′⟩ 73 times, ⟨a⟩ 17 times, ⟨i⟩ before *yod* 6 times, elsewhere (never before a laryngeal or after *yod*) 4 times, ⟨o⟩ once (9r31). These numbers alone are sufficient contrast to the usage described for folios 12v–14v, but apart from that, the earlier folios and TS H16:9 show no trace of the special use of signs for *shewa* vowels before laryngeals described below.

124 Some 207 times. It is also the most common sign used where bA would have either *segol* or *ṣere*.

125 Some 42 times. This sign is used only where bA would have *shewa*. From Murtonen's description (1958, p. 30) I take it that this sign (his no. 3) is the work of some hand later than the original, which, in the sporadic fashion sometimes found in Palestinian mss., made some additions to, and some changes in (Murtonen's no. 4), the original. Cf. the use of ⟨e′⟩ and the combination of ⟨e⟩ and ⟨e′⟩ in TS 12:197. See also note 131.

126 12v11, 12, 29. In no case is the vowel following the *'alef* marked. The first two instances are quoted by Murtonen (1958, p. 25) as evidence of the quiescence

twice where bA would have *'alef* or *he* followed by *ḥireq*,[127] and elsewhere only where bA would have *shewa* before *yod* (a typical Palestinian spelling), or after *yod* (less typical but still well attested in other mss.). ⟨e′⟩ is used 10 times where bA would have *shewa* before *'alef* or *he* followed by *ṣere*, and corresponds to *shewa* in only six other cases.[128] Similar cases can be noted in which ⟨a⟩ and ⟨a′⟩ are used where bA would have *shewa* before *'alef* or *he* followed by 'a' vowels, but both these signs are also used where bA uses *shewa* in other positions.[129] The fact that the *'alef* or *he* in most of these cases is pointed with a vowel sign seems to me sufficient guarantee that it is not quiescent in any of these cases.[130]

12 These cases in which *'alef* or *he* separates the two vowels in

---

of *'alef*, but in view of the evidence for the use of ⟨e′⟩ and ⟨i⟩ in this position, I do not think his view can be maintained.

127 12v16, 23. In 12v16 the vowel following the *'alef* is marked as ⟨i⟩. In 14r2 a '*shewa* vowel' in this position is marked by ⟨e⟩, not ⟨i⟩.

128 Before *'alef*, 12v17, 20, 13r14, 13v15, 14r18, 20, 27. Before *he*, 12v8, 13r2, 14r7. In all these cases the *'alef* or *he* is pointed with ⟨e⟩ (the sign most commonly used where bA has *ṣere*), except 14r27, where no sign is written, and 14r18 where ⟨a′⟩ is used, in my opinion by error. In 13v24 a '*shewa* vowel' in this position is marked by ⟨e⟩, not ⟨e′⟩.

129 Where bA would have *shewa* before *'alef* or *he* followed by *qameṣ*, this ms. has ⟨a⟩ in 13r15, 33 and 13v4 and ⟨a′⟩ in 13v16; the same followed by *pataḥ*: ⟨a′⟩ 12v3, 19, 26, 13r3, 10, 13v2, 31, 14r4. In these instances the vowel following the *'alef* or *he* is marked with ⟨a′⟩ 7 times and with ⟨a⟩ 3 times, and is not marked twice. Only in 14v14 is a '*shewa* vowel' in this position marked by ⟨e⟩. It is interesting to note that the same phenomenon apparently extends to '*shewa* vowels' before *ḥet* and *'ayin* followed by 'a' vowels. In this case the '*shewa* vowel' is always marked ⟨a′⟩. The following bA vowel would be *qameṣ* in 12v17, 13v17, 14r14, 20 and *pataḥ* in 14r5, 14v4, 6, 10, 10. The vowel following the *'ayin* or *ḥet* is marked as ⟨a′⟩ 5 times, ⟨a⟩ 4 times. A '*shewa* vowel' in this position is marked by ⟨e⟩ (13r18) and ≤ (13r15) both before bA *'ayin* followed by *qameṣ*. Elsewhere ⟨a⟩ is used 20 times where bA would have *shewa*, and ⟨a′⟩ 31 times.

130 For examples see notes 127–9. One might object that in 12v17 the infinitive form ⟨š't⟩ is written with vowel signs over both *śin* and *'alef*, but also with the 'Pal. *rafe* sign' ᵕ over the *'alef*. Murtonen (1958, p. 33) states that this sign indicates that the *'alef* is quiescent. The sign may be used to mark a laryngeal as quiescent, as shown, e.g., in Kahle, 1901, p. 307. In no case where it is used in this way does the laryngeal in question carry a vowel sign. The same sign is also used to indicate that a laryngeal, or *waw* or *yod* had a consonantal value, as in Bod. Heb. d63 f. 98 (Murtonen, 1958. p. 33), and TS 12:195+ (Kahle, 1930, p. 29* – also *yod*, Ps. 52:8 – and Dietrich, 1960, p. 71). It should be noted that the marking of '*shewa* vowels' in the latter ms. is very similar to that in Bod. Heb. d55 f. 12v–14v (see note 132). There is therefore at least good reason to doubt that the *'alef* in question is quiescent. (On Murtonen's argument from the writing of one vowel sign only by the first hand (cf. 12v4) see note 133.) It seems to me likely that the use of '*rafe*' in this position may indicate a different type of pronunciation from the normal (i.e. *'alef* may here represent a palatalized stop or 'offglide' /y/ rather than quiescence).

question can be paralleled by ones in which some other consonant appears in this position, and where ⟨e⟩ or ⪯ corresponds to the bA *shewa*. We must, then, be dealing with '*shewa* vowels,' which, before *'alef* or *he*, were pronounced with the quality of the vowel following the consonant in question. In this ms. the vocalizer indicated the quality required. This parallels the rule given by the early grammarians, with the exception that they state that *shewa* before any laryngeal has the quality of the vowel following the laryngeal, not, for all but 'a' vowels, solely before *'alef* and *he* as in this ms.[131] This care in the indication of '*shewa* vowel' quality is not, so far as I know, carried so far in any other ms., but there are other examples.[132] The fact that *'alef* and *he* are often shown as separating two vowel sounds, either of the same or of different qualities, and the obvious distinction between these two and the other laryngeals, should make scholars more cautious in assuming the breakdown of the Palestinian laryngeal system.[133]

131 See, e.g., Derenbourg, 1870, p. 369; Qimḥi, 1842, p. 138b; Skoss, 1955, p. 31; Nutt, 1870, p. 130; Ginsburg, 1897, p. 988, no. 14 (his edition of a form of *Diqduqe haṬə'amim*; the fuller Baer-Strack edition is not available to me) and the information given by Levy, 1936, pp. 17* and 30. I have noted only one instance of the use of a sign where bA would have *shewa* before a laryngeal followed by *shureq*. The sign here is ⪯ (13v3). This could mean that the rule did not hold in the case of 'u' vowels, but this sign shows a number of exceptions to the general usage of the ms. (e.g., it marks a '*shewa* vowel' before *yod* in 13r19 and 13v22, a position where ⟨i⟩ usually occurs – see preceding paragraph – and ⟨e⟩ never does) and is probably a secondary addition to the original pointing (see note 125). Writings such as ⟨*ḥṭw'w*⟩ in TS H16:10 v2 (15:23) might indicate that a '*shewa* vowel' did take on a 'u' colouring in this position. For the probability that the rule applied to '*shewa* vowels' before any laryngeal followed by an 'a' vowel, see note 129. That it does not apply to '*shewa* vowels' before *ḥet* or *'ayin* followed by other vowels is shown, e.g. where bA would have following *ḥolem*, 13r6, 14r2; *ṣere*, 12v24, 26, 29; *ḥireq*, 14v18.

132 TS 12:195+ shows almost as complete a system, but with some differences, principally that the rules for this 'harmonization' of '*shewa* vowels' seem to apply with any laryngeal followed by any vowel. ⟨o⟩ is used before bA *'alef* and *ḥet* followed by *ḥolem*, Pss. 55:12, 69:37; ⟨a⟩ before *'alef*, *he*, or *ḥet* followed by an 'a' vowel, Pss. 55:11, 15, 69:28, 77:18, elsewhere only Ps. 70:3; ⟨a'⟩ before bA *'alef* or *he* followed by *pataḥ*, Pss. 52:9, 55:14, and nowhere else. ⟨e'⟩ is not used before a laryngeal. ⟨e⟩ is the sign normally used in this ms. where bA has *shewa* (80 cases). ⟨i⟩ is used before bA *he* followed by *ḥireq*, Pss. 53:2, 71:6, 8, and elsewhere before or after *yod* (6 cases). Other mss. show occasional examples, e.g. TS A43:1, Jer. 25:6, 11.

133 Murtonen, 1964, argues (pp. 14–15, amplifying former arguments) that the 'first hand' did not pronounce the laryngeals while the second did. He bases this on the fact that the first hand wrote no vowel signs in certain positions. However, in a text in which all vowels are not marked, no significance can be attached to the absence of a vowel sign. Kahle's argument from the fact that words ending in different laryngeals are used as rhymes (Kahle, 1959, p. 167) is equally weak, as the *payyeṭanim* obviously did not mind inexact rhymes as long as the 'rhyming' sounds were reasonably close; e.g. Kahle, 1927, Heb. p. 8, poem v, l. 4, ⟨*b*⟩ 'rhymes

13 Another example of the evident similarity of the Palestinian pronunciation of '*shewa* vowels' to that prescribed for bA in special situations occurs where bA has *shewa* before *yod*. The early grammarians state that, in this position, the '*shewa* vowel' has the quality of *ḥireq*.[134] The fact that the Palestinians wrote ⟨i⟩ in this position is one of the best-known characteristics of their system. The probability, if not the fact, that this ⟨i⟩ represents a '*shewa* vowel' may be established by comparing the forms in which it occurs[135] with forms in the same ms. involving consonants other than *yod*. The vowel in question will be seen to be written with whatever sign is commonly in that ms. where bA uses *shewa*. Some mss., however, do not consistently use ⟨i⟩ where bA would have *shewa* before *yod*.[136] Some Palestinian mss. also occasionally write ⟨i⟩ where bA would have *shewa* after *yod*, a pointing which, as far as I know, finds no parallel in the descriptions of the early grammarians.[137] These

with' ⟨l⟩, so ⟨m⟩ with ⟨n⟩ 9.II.11 etc. Examples are not uncommon in Yannai; e.g. Murtonen, 1958, ms. d, 2v22 (cf. p. 28 on *'ayin*). There is really very little evidence for the loss of laryngeal consonants. The note in *Jer. Berakhoth* 2:4 describes only the fact that the original four laryngeal phonemes have been reduced, in some areas, to two (presumably phonemic) sounds; *'ayin/'alef*, pronounced as the author of the note pronounced *'alef*, and *he/ḥet* pronounced as he pronounced *ḥet*. This, as a decree concerning ceremonial reading of the Bible, is certainly the most important of the various statements on pronunciation. The stories in *Bab. 'Erubin* 53b contradict this view, but the confusion of sounds suggested there is so great that I take them as good, but not true, stories. There was a second type of change in the original system which apparently left three 'phonemes': *'ayin*, *ḥet*, and *he/'alef*. This is found in most of the Qumran scrolls, where *he* appears to be completely quiescent in a few specific positions (e.g. in the *hif'il* infinitive after *lamed*), and elsewhere interchanges a good deal with *'alef*. Probably the sounds indicated by *he* and *'alef* were virtually identical, but there is no reason to suppose that they had no consonantal value in most positions. There is almost no evidence outside 1QIs[a] for the general confusion of the sounds represented by *he*, *ḥet*, and *'ayin*. Presumably the author of the note in *Berakot* used this 'three laryngeal system.' It also seems to have been used by the author of the ms. discussed here. Evidence of it can be seen in bA, but those who believe that the Masoretes 'restored' a lost laryngeal system by the use of *ḥaṭef* vowels have yet to explain contrasts such as the vocalization of the preposition in *be'lohiym* and *bɛ'ĕmɛt*.

134 See, e.g., Derenbourg, 1870, p. 370; Qimḥi, 1842, pp. 138b–139a; Skoss, 1955, p. 32; Nutt, 1870, p. 131; Ginsburg, 1897, p. 999, no. 42; Levy, 1936, p. 25* and p. 30.

135 The most common occurrences are where one of the prepositions *b-*, *k-*, or *l-*, or the conjunction *w-*, precedes a word beginning with *yod*.

136 E.g., TS 16:96 and TS 12:195+. In general, mss. which do not use the 'a' signs as bA uses *qameṣ* and *pataḥ* do not use ⟨i⟩ consistently where bA uses *shewa* before *yod*.

137 Pal. usage never appears consistent, e.g. Bod. Heb. d55 f. 12v16, 25, 14r14, 14v25, but cf. 12v22, 30, 14r26, 14v12, 29, where ⟨i⟩ is not used. In a ms. as carefully pointed as this one appears to be, it seems reasonable to suppose that this would reflect a real difference in pronunciation. ⟨i⟩ also occasionally appears where in bA the *shewa* would be quiescent, e.g. in TS H2:1 r14, after the first *nun* in *'inyɔniym*.

small differences merely serve to underline the general similarity.

14 It is also possible to demonstrate that Pal. must have used '*shewa* vowels' in at least some cases where bA has composite *shewa* signs. Pal. normally uses ⟨a′⟩ (less commonly ⟨a⟩) where bA has *ḥaṭef pataḥ*. In a number of cases, however, ⟨e⟩ or ⟨e′⟩ is used in this position. These signs undoubtedly indicate the use of a simple *shewa* sound, rather than a specifically coloured one (see § 1.36). It would be possible to use a similar argument where ⟨a′⟩ or ⟨e′⟩ is used where bA has *ḥaṭef segol*. In the overwhelming majority of cases, however, ⟨e⟩ is used in this position. Other signs are so rare that they can probably be taken as representing errors or variant forms. Where bA has *ḥaṭef qameṣ* Pal. normally uses ⟨a⟩. This shows that the vowel sound used in these positions differed from that used where bA has *qameṣ ḥaṭuf*, where Pal. normally uses ⟨o⟩. The difference was certainly one of quality, but very likely one of quantity as well (see § 1.32). ⟨o⟩ is used in a few cases where bA has *ḥaṭef qameṣ*. Its use here probably indicates that the vowel in question was not of *shewa* quantity.[138] ⟨a′⟩ is used where bA has *ḥaṭef qameṣ* in mss. which use ⟨a⟩ and ⟨a′⟩ indiscriminately in most other situations as well. Its use here is presumably symptomatic of that confusion.

15 The examples given in 4–14 above show that there must have been great similarity between the Palestinian use and pronunciation of '*shewa* vowels' and that described by the grammarians for such vowels as indicated by bA. The major difference is the fact that the Palestinian vocalizers, if they wished to indicate such vowels at all, had to indicate the exact quality to be used, whereas such complexity and detail in the indication of '*shewa* vowels' was never needed in bA because the *shewa* sign was not tied to any vowel quality. It is not to be imagined, however, that it is claimed that the two pointing systems indicated identical pronunciation. In most mss. there are a few exceptions which disrupt the general pattern of the use of signs. Some examples are mentioned in notes 117, 123, 125, 127, 128, 129, 137. Some of these may well be due to differences between Palestinian pronunciation and that of bA.

16 In addition to such irregularities, there are cases in which the Palestinian pointing commonly uses some unusual sign where bA has *shewa*. An example is the fairly common use of ⟨a⟩ where bA

138 In מחלי TS K26:8, II Kings 8:8, and a few other nouns of the same form. Cf., e.g., bA *mɛšiy*, *pɛtiy*, with forms such as *kəliy*.

has *shewa* in third person masculine pural and similar verb forms; particularly, it seems, from passive stems.[139] Such cases occur over a wide range of mss., and must certainly indicate a difference between Palestinian pronunciation and that of bA, probably a difference dependent on different intonation patterns.

17 Finally one can raise the question of the Palestinian use of a vowel sign where bA uses a *shewa* which is commonly regarded as 'silent.' Murtonen is of course correct when he points out that, in a system which does not use a sign to indicate every vowel, there can be no question of the use of any vowel sign to indicate the absence of a vowel.[140] Consequently there are cases in which the Palestinians pronounced a vowel where bA, to the best of our knowledge, did not. In one case at least, such pronunciation seems to be indicated, though inconsistently, in a number of mss., and so must probably be regarded as characteristic of at least a section of those who used the Palestinian pointing. The case is the *shewa* before the *taw* of the second person masculine singular pronominal element of the perfect verb form. In a number of cases, in a number of mss., a vowel sign (usually ⟨a′⟩) is written before this *taw*. This phenomenon does not appear to occur widely enough to be considered a characteristic of all Palestinian Hebrew, but, whatever the significance of the vowel sign, it would appear to indicate a definite difference from the pronunciation of bA.[141]

18 Murtonen's attitude towards the existence of '*shewa* vowels' in Palestinian Hebrew as expressed in his *Materials for a Non-Masoretic Hebrew Grammar*, vol. I,[142] and apparently retained in vol. III,[143] seems to me to stress much too heavily the possible differences, rather than the probable similarities, between the Palestinian pronunciation and that of ben Asher. He does give a

139 A few examples are given in Murtonen, 1958, pp. 38, 42, 44. Other examples are also mostly from non-biblical mss., e.g. Ant. 369, 2r9, 22, 29, 29, 30, 30, 30 (18:12, 19:8, 15, 16), but biblical examples do occur: e.g. TS 12:197, Dan. 12:10.

140 Murtonen, 1958, p. 39. The '*rafe* sign' is used to indicate a quiescent consonant (i.e. the absence of a following vowel); see note 130.

141 E.g., Bod. ms. Heb. d55 f. 4r11, 12, 13, 14, 15, 16, etc. It is difficult to evaluate such forms, as the placing of vowel signs is often careless. Contrasting forms appear in the same lines. This, like so many features of Palestinian pointing, also appears in non-bA Tiberian mss. Cf. one noted by Díez-Macho, 1963b, p. 249, Judg. 9:33 (TS NS 281:2). (See p. 241 on the use of *pataḥ* where bA uses *shewa*, and p. 239 for a different explanation of this form.)

142 (1958) in his notes on the vowel signs, pp. 29ff. Especially: "It is naturally possible that they [Palestinian vowel signs] in some places actually represent a sound like Tib. *Ḥaṭef* or *Shwa*, but too exact rules in this respect are artificial" (p. 29).

143 1964, pp. 13–14.

necessary caution against the making of exact rules,[144] which must always be borne in mind. There were definitely differences between the Palestinian use of '*shewa* vowels' and that of bA, but these do not appear to have been numerous.[145] The information given here would seem to show that the use and – as far as can be determined – the pronunciation of '*shewa* vowels' in Palestinian Hebrew was much the same as that described by the early grammarians as used in the Hebrew of bA.[146]

APPENDIX A

MANUSCRIPTS REFERRED TO IN THIS STUDY

This list includes all published Palestinian mss., and also unpublished Palestinian and other mss. mentioned in this study. Where several different fragments belong to the same text, they are listed under the first fragment of that text, or the first fragment to be published. The text as a whole is quoted by that number followed by a plus sign.[147] All the mss. listed have Palestinian pointing unless otherwise noted.

A complete listing of unpublished mss., together with a fuller description, appears in HTPV. Of the unpublished texts listed here, those containing poems by Yannai (with the exception of H.U.C. ms. 1001 and TS NS 249:7) have been briefly described in Zulay (1936). Those in the T-S New Series were discovered by Dr. Manfried Dietrich, who has very kindly allowed me to use all the materials he had gathered, for which I am very grateful. This study has benefitted greatly from the many discussions of the Palestinian pointing which I have had with him.

144 See note 142.

145 This is shown, among other things, by the fact that, all told, the number of vowel signs used in Palestinian mss. where bA has silent *shewa* is extremely small. For instance, I would say that Heb. d55 f. 12v–14v has no more than 10 cases: ⟨a′⟩ 12v18, 13r8, 13v9, 14r12, 14v2, 6, 6, 9; ⟨e⟩ 13v2; ≤ 13v5. Again possible examples are often difficult to evaluate, as the placing of signs is often careless. The full extent of such differences cannot, of course, be known until a complete morphology of Pal. is drawn up.

146 It could be argued that the testimony of the grammarians is derived from local pronunciation, or from the works of other scholars. Both objections may be valid to some extent, but it should be noted that the authorities quoted in notes 131 and 134 come from different areas, and all give similar, but not identical testimony.

147 The text listed as H.U.C. ms. 1001+ is made an exception, because the 'Levias fragment' is now lost.

(i) *Mss. in the Taylor-Schechter collection of the University Library, Cambridge*

TS 12:195 + 196 + TS NS 249:3 Kahle, 1930, MS L; Dietrich 1960, ms. Cb 8.

TS 12:196 See TS 12:195.

TS 12:197 Kahle, 1930, ms. K.

TS 12: 210 See TS NS 249:14.

TS 16:93 Allony and Díez-Macho, 1959.

TS 16:96 Kahle, 1930, ms. J.

TS 20:53 + 54 + 58 + 52 Murtonen, 1958, ms. c (see also *ibid.* 1964, pp. 16f.); Allony and Díez-Macho, 1958*a*, 1958*b*, 1959. The slight differences in pointing between the fragments are not considered sufficiently important to warrant treating them as separate mss.

TS 20:59 + TS 2nd 1:125 Kahle, 1930, ms. H; Dietrich, 1960, ms. Cb 5.

TS A43:1 See Bod. Heb. e30f. 48–9.

TS B6:2 Díez-Macho, 1963*a*, pp. 36f. 'Ben Naftali.'

TS B17:25 Yeivin, 1963.

TS D1:12 Weil, 1962.

TS E1:95 Unpublished Mishna fragment: parts of *Nazir* and *Soṭa*. Thoroughgoing Tiberian pointing in a style which does not use *qameṣ* or *segol*, but is sufficiently sophisticated to use composite *shewa* signs (*pataḥ* r10, 17 etc., *ṣere* r23, 23, etc.)

TS E1:107 Allony, 1963.

TS H2:1 Unpublished. Poems of Yannai. Thoroughgoing pointing. Recto and verso are vocalized differently.

TS H2:2 See TS H16:3.

TS H2:29 Unpublished. Poems by Yehuda Zebida. The vocalization is fairly thouroughgoing. The system (see note 11) is, as far as I know, unique.

TS H2:30 Unpublished. Passover liturgy. On paper. Palestinian vocalization fairly thoroughgoing, complemented by Tiberian.

TS H5:25 Edelmann, 1934, ms. D_1.

TS H5:222 Unpublished. Liturgy for Day of Atonement. Sparsely pointed.

TS H6:51 See TS NS 117:7.

TS H7:1 Unpublished. Qalir. Liturgy for Tabernacles. Sparsely pointed.

TS H7:7 Unpublished. Poems of Yannai. Vocalization thoroughgoing.

TS H16:1 + TS NS 249:1 Edelmann, 1934, ms F. The New Series fragment (unpublished) is small and badly preserved, but completes the height of the page.

TS H16:2 See TS H16:3.

TS H16:3 + TS H16:2 + Bod. Heb. d63 f. 82–9 + TS H2:2 + TS NS 249:12 Kahle, 1927. The last two fragments named are unpublished.

TS H16:4 Murtonen, 1958, ms. e.

TS H16:5 Edelmann, 1934, ms. G.

TS H16:6 Edelmann, 1934, ms. A.

TS H16:7 Kober, 1929. (See Ant. 369.)
TS H16:8 Edelmann, 1934, ms. B.
TS H16:9 + Bod. Heb. d55 f. 4r–7v, 9r–12r Edelmann, 1934, ms. C; Murtonen, 1958, ms. a (1st part, see note 123).
TS H16:10 Edelmann, 1934, ms. D.
TS H16:12 + Bod. Heb. c20 f. 5–6 Parts of both fragments are published in Zulay, 1936, pp. 222–8.
TS K25:108 See Bod. Heb. e30 f. 48–9.
TS K26:1 Dietrich, 1960, ms. Cb 2.
TS K26:8 See Bod. Heb. d44 f. 1–4.
TS 13H2:10 Murtonen, 1958, ms. d.
TS 13H2:11 + TS 13H2:12 Unpublished. Poems of Yannai. Sparsely pointed.
TS 13H2:12 See TS 13H2:11.

TS 2nd Series[148]

TS 2nd 1:44 Dietrich, 1960, ms. Cb 4.
TS 2nd 1:125 See TS 20:59.
TS 2nd 1:130 Dietrich, 1960, ms. Cb 6.
TS 2nd 2:71 Dietrich, 1960, ms. Cb 7.

TS New Series

TS NS 42:1 Unpublished. Parts of Job sparsely pointed with Tiberian points in a system similar to that of Bod. Heb. c20 f. 25–8 and TS E1:95. This ms was discovered, and is, I believe, to be published by Professor Díez-Macho, who very kindly drew my attention to it.
TS NS 117:7 + TS H6:51 Unpublished. Liturgy for the Day of Atonement. Sparsely pointed.
TS NS 119:42 Unpublished. Liturgy for the ninth of Ab. Sparsely pointed.
TS NS 249:1 See TS H16:1.
TS NS 249:3 See TS 12:195.
TS NS 249:5 See Bod. Heb. e30 f. 48–9.
TS NS 249:6 Dietrich, 1960, ms. Cb 9.
TS NS 249:7 See H.U.C. ms. 1001.
TS NS 249:8[149] + TS NS 281:2 Dietrich, 1960, ms. Cb 10; Díez-Macho, 1963*b*.
TS NS 249:9 See Bod. Heb. e30 f. 48–9.
TS NS 249:12 See TS H16:3.
TS NS 249:14 + TS 12:210 Unpublished. Qalir. Passover liturgy. Thoroughgoing pointing in a unique system.
TS NS 281:2 See TS NS 249:8.

148 The numbers in the TS second series under which Dr. Dietrich published these texts are now apparently obsolete, but I have not so far been able to trace the present numbers of these texts.

149 This is the number under which Dr. Dietrich published this text, but it has since been changed, and I have so far not been able to trace the present number.

(ii) *Mss. from the collection of the Bodleian Library, Oxford*

Bod. Heb. c20 f. 5–6 See TS H16:12.
Bod. Heb. c20 f. 25–8 Described by Díez-Macho, 1963*a*, as ms. 31 (see note 72). 'Ben Naftali.'
Bod. Heb. d29 f. 17–20 Dietrich, 1960, ms. Ob 1.
Bod. Heb. d37 f. 38–9 See Bod. Heb. d44 f. 1–4.
Bod. Heb. d41 f. 11–15 The pointing of f. 15v and 15r 1–15 is published in Bar, 1936.
Bod. Heb. d44 f. 1–4 + Bod. Heb. d37 f. 38–9 + TS K26:8 Dietrich, 1960, ms. Ob2/Cb3.
Bod. Heb. d55 f. 4r–7v, 9r–12r See TS H16:9.
Bod. Heb. d55 f. 12v–14v Murtonen, 1958, ms. a, 2nd part (see note 123).
Bod. Heb. d63 f. 82–9 See TS H16:3.
Bod. Heb. d63 f. 98 The verso is published in Murtonen, 1958, as ms. b.
Bod. Heb. e30 f. 48–9 + TS A43:1 + TS K25:108 + TS NS 249:5 + TS NS 249:9 Kahle, 1901, 1930, ms. M; Dietrich, 1960, ms. Cb 1.

(iii) *Mss. in the collection of the Library of the Jewish Theological Seminary of America, New York*

J.T.S. ms. 504 f. 2 Díez-Macho, 1954. The pointing of further leaves from the same ms. is described in Yeivin, 1963.
J.T.S. ms. 594 box B, env. 12 Kahle, 1959, pp. 338–44.

(iv) *Mss. in the collection of the Hebrew Union College, Cincinnati*

H.U.C. 'Levias' See H.U.C. ms. 1001.
H.U.C. ms. 1001 + H.U.C. 'Levias' + TS NS 249:7. The first-named fragment is partially published in Sonne, 1944. The pointing given there, which is transcribed into Tiberian signs, is inadequate. I have used for this study a transcription made jointly by Dr. Dietrich and myself from a photograph. The 'Levias' fragment is unfortunately now lost. It was published in Levias, 1899, and this edition was copied in Kahle, 1927. The TS New Series fragment is unpublished.

(v) *Mss. in the Antonin Collection of the Saltykov-Shchedrin State Public Library, Leningrad*

Ant. 222 Murtonen, 1958, ms. f.
Ant. 369 Kober, 1929. Published as part of TS H16:7. I have listed them separately here on the ground of slight differences in the use of the 'e' signs.
Ant. 912 Ormann, 1934.
Ant. 959 Edelmann, 1934, ms. E.

APPENDIX B

THE USE OF 'A' AND 'E' SIGNS IN THE MSS. STUDIED IN § 1.8–12

These statistics refer only to the use of ⟨a⟩ and ⟨a′⟩ corresponding to bA *qameṣ* and *pataḥ*, and of ⟨e⟩ and ⟨e′⟩ corresponding to bA *segol and ṣere*. The ten columns contain information as follows:

1 Total uses of ⟨a⟩ and ⟨a′⟩ corresponding to bA *qameṣ* and *pataḥ*.
2 Percentage of those vowels represented by ⟨a⟩.
3 Percentage of those uses of ⟨a⟩ corresponding to bA *qameṣ*.
4 Percentage of total 'a' vowels represented by ⟨a′⟩.
5 Percentage of those uses of ⟨a′⟩ corresponding to bA *qameṣ*.
6 Total uses of ⟨e⟩ and ⟨e′⟩ corresponding to bA *segol* and *ṣere*.
7 Percentage of those vowels represented by ⟨e⟩.
8 Percentage of those uses of ⟨e⟩ corresponding to bA *ṣere*.
9 Percentage of total 'e' vowels represented by ⟨e′⟩.
10 Percentage of uses of ⟨e′⟩ corresponding to bA *ṣere*.

	1	2	3	4	5	6	7	8	9	10
TS 12:195+	404	76	71	24	21	211	75	51	25	40
TS 16:93	–	–	–	–	–	32	44	21	56	56
TS 16:96	263	86	61	14	34	–	–	–	–	–
TS 20:53+	334	22	90	78	56	141	58	49	42	53
TS 20:59+	–	–	–	–	–	102	30	42	70	75
TS E1:107	–	–	–	–	–	20	80	50	20	25
TS H5:222	–	–	–	–	–	19	53	20	47	78
TS H16:1+	194	54	81	46	42	–	–	–	–	–
TS H16:3+[150]	366	67	75	33	42	–	–	–	–	–
TS H16:5	108	52	79	48	52	–	–	–	–	–
TS H16:6	–	–	–	–	–	108	21	39	79	59
TS H16:7	–	–	–	–	–	83	82	35	18	78
TS H16:8	340	61	65	39	44	–	–	–	–	–
TS H16:9+[151]	628	67	75	33	46	–	–	–	–	–
TS K26:1	24	75	39	25	67	–	–	–	–	–
TS 2nd 1:130	6	33	50	67	100	–	–	–	–	–
TS NS 119:42	–	–	–	–	–	11	82	67	18	50
TS NS 249:6	–	–	–	–	–	29	72	24	28	88
TS NS 249:8+	15	80	75	20	33	15	60	22	40	83
Bod. Heb. d29 f. 17–20	193	69	85	31	32	–	–	–	–	–
Bod. Heb. d41 f. 15[152]	232	68	82	32	38	–	–	–	–	–
Bod. Heb. d55 f. 12v–14v[153]	–	–	–	–	–	133	95	40	5	100
Bod. Heb. d63 f. 98	–	–	–	–	–	55	65	36	35	89
J.T.S. ms. 594 box B, env. 12	–	–	–	–	–	44	68	20	32	82
Ant. 222	50	40	85	60	27	–	–	–	–	–
Ant. 369	–	–	–	–	–	95	60	37	40	67
Ant. 912	621	52	73	48	37	–	–	–	–	–

150 These figures are from TS H16:3 taken as a sample.
151 These figures are from Bod. Heb. d55 f. 4–5 only.
152 These figures represent only the part of the text published by Bar (1936).
153 These figures are from fols. 12v–13 only.

APPENDIX C

THE OCCURRENCE OF THE COMMON DIVERGENT USES OF SIGNS

The numbers along the top of the table indicate that the syllable in which the usage occurs is:

1 Stressed, closed, final.
2 Stressed, open, final.
3 Stressed, open, non-final.
4 Unstressed, open.
5 Unstressed, open or closed, vowel preceding a laryngeal.
6 Unstressed, closed, vowel preceding a doubled consonant.
7 Unstressed, closed.
8 Unstressed, closed, final.

Usage		1	2	3	4	5	6	7	8
⟨o⟩	= *shureq*	24	20	–	15	8	23	2	–
⟨u⟩	= *ḥolem*	14	17	1	25	–	–	–	–
⟨a′⟩	= *qameṣ*[154]	55	30	1	38	8	–	–	–
⟨e/e′⟩	= *qameṣ*[155]	4	7	4	29	–	–	1	–
⟨a⟩	= *pataḥ*[154]	68	–	–	16	16	22	25	–
⟨e⟩	= *pataḥ*	4	–	–	2	18	1	12	12
⟨e′⟩	= *segol*[156]	4	1	1	–	2	1	1	1
⟨a′⟩	= *segol*	4	–	5	–	2	–	9	5
⟨i⟩	= *segol*	–	1	2	–	6	2	6	1
⟨e⟩	= *ṣere*[156]	3	–	3	1	–	–	–	–
⟨a′⟩	= *ṣere*	29	1	–	–	–	–	–	1
⟨a⟩	= *ṣere*	17	–	3	1	–	–	–	–
⟨i⟩	= *ṣere*	8	5	1	15	3	–	–	–
⟨e/e′⟩	= *ḥireq*[157]	17	10	2	14	27	25	25	–
⟨a′⟩	= *ḥireq*	1	–	–	2	–	2	9	–

REFERENCES

Allony, N. 1963. "A Fragment of Mishna with Palestinian Pointing," in *Sefer haYobel leRabbi Hanok Yalon*. Jerusalem.

Allony, N. and Díez-Macho, A. 1958*a*. "Otros dos manuscritos 'palestinenses,'" *Sefarad* 18, pp. 254–71.

— 1958*b*. "Dos manuscritos 'palestinenses' más de la Geniza del Cairo," *Estudios Biblicos* 17, pp. 83–100.

— 1959. "A Fragment of Pesikta de Rav Kahana with Palestinian Vocalization," *Leshonenu* 23, pp. 57–71.

154 This information is taken only from mss. of classes 1, 2, 4, and 6.

155 ⟨e′⟩ only in ustressed, open syllables, 11 cases.

156 This information is taken only from mss. of class 1.

157 Because of its peculiar use of ⟨i⟩ and ⟨e′⟩, Bod. Heb. d63 f. 98 was not used here. Also omitted are those special cases where ⟨e⟩ or ⟨e′⟩ is used where bA has *ḥireq* in the 'diphtong' *-ayi-* (TS 20:59, Ezek. 16:11; Bod. Heb. d41 f. 11–15, three times; Bod. Heb. d44 f. 1–4+, *passim*).

Bar, F. 1936. *Liturgische Dichtungen von Jannai und Samuel.* Bonn.
Bauer-Leander. 1922. *Historische Grammatik der hebräischen Sprache des alten Testaments.* Halle.
Ben David, A. 1958. Review of Murtonen, 1958, in *Kirjath Sepher* 33, pp. 482–91.
Ben Hayyim, Z. 1953. "R. Saadya Ga'on's theory of Vowels," *Leshonenu* 18, pp. 89–96.
— 1954*a*. *Studies in the Traditions of the Hebrew Language.* Madrid.
— 1954*b*. "The Samaritan Vowel System and Its Graphic Representation," *Archiv Orientální* 22, pp. 515–30.
Bét-Aryé, M. 1965. "The Vocalization of the Worms Maḥzor," *Leshonenu* 29, pp. 27–39, 80–102.
Brønno, E. 1943. *Studien über hebräische Morphologie und Vokalismus* (Abhandlungen für die Kunde des Morgenlandes XXVIII). Leipzig.
Derenbourg, M. J. 1870. "Manuel du lecteur," *Journal asiatique*, 6e série, 16.
Dietrich, M. 1960. "Neue palästinisch punktierte Bibelfragmente." Thesis, Tübingen.
— 1968. *Neue palästinisch punktierte Bibelfragmente.* Leiden.
Díez-Macho, A. 1954. "Tres nuevos MSS 'palestinenses,'" *Estudios Biblicos* 13, pp. 247–65.
— 1963*a*. "A New List of So-called 'Ben-Naftali' Manuscripts," in *Hebrew and Semitic Studies Presented to G. R. Driver.* Oxford.
— 1963*b*. "Un nuevo ms. 'palestinense' del libro de Jueces ...," *Sefarad* 23, pp. 236–51.
Edelmann, R. 1934. *Zur Frühgeschichte des Maḥzor* (Bonner orientalistische Studien, Heft 6). Stuttgart.
Garbell, I. 1959. "The Phonemic Status of *Shewa* etc.," *Leshonenu* 23, pp. 152–5.
Gesenius-Kautzch. 1910. *Gesenius' Hebrew Grammar*, edited, etc. by E. Kautzch. Second English edition, Oxford.
Ginsburg, C. D. 1897. *Introduction to the Massoretico-Critical Edition of the Hebrew Bible.* London.
Goshen-Gottstein, M. 1963. "The Rise of the Tiberian Bible Text," in *Biblical and Other Studies*, ed. A. Altmann. Cambridge, Mass.
Kahle, P. 1901. "Beiträge zur Geschichte der hebräischen Punktation," *ZAW* 21, pp. 273–317.
— 1913. *Masoreten des Ostens.* Leipzig.
— 1927. *Masoreten des Westens I.* Stuttgart.
— 1930. *Masoreten des Westens II.* Stuttgart.
— 1959. *The Cairo Geniza.* Oxford.
Kober, M. 1929. *Zum Machzor Jannai.* Frankfurt a. M.
Levias, C. 1899. "The Palestinian Vocalization," *AJSL* 15, pp. 157-64.
Levy, K. 1936. *Zur masoretischen Grammatik* (Bonner orientalistische Studien, Heft 15). Stuttgart.
McIntosh, A. 1956. "The Analysis of Written Middle English," *Transactions of the Philological Society* 1956, pp. 26–55.

Morag, S. 1959. "The Vocalization of the Codex Reuchlinianus," *JSS* 4, pp. 216–37.

— 1962. *The Vocalization Systems of Arabic, Hebrew, and Aramaic.* 's-Gravenhage.

— 1963. *The Hebrew Language Tradition of the Yemenite Jews.* Jerusalem.

— 1965. "Remarks on the Description of the Vocalization of the Worms Maḥzor," *Leshonenu* 29, pp. 203–9.

Murtonen, A. 1958. *Materials for a Non-Masoretic Hebrew Grammar*, vol. I. Helsinki.

— 1964. *Materials for a Non-Masoretic Hebrew Grammar*, vol. III (Studia Orientalia ed. Soc. Or. Fennica XXIX). Helsinki.

Nutt, J. W. 1870. *Two Treatises on Verbs etc. by R. Jehuda Hayug of Fez ...* London.

Ormann, G. 1934. *Das Sündenbekenntnis des Versöhnungstages.* Frankfurt a. M.

Porath, E. 1938. *Mishnaic Hebrew as Vocalized in the Early Manuscripts of the Babylonian Jews.* Jerusalem.

Qimḥi, D. 1842. *Miklol*, ed. Rittenberg. Lyk.

Schramm, G. 1964. *The Graphemes of Tiberian Hebrew.* Berkeley.

Segal, M. H. 1927. *A Grammar of Mishnaic Hebrew.* Oxford.

Skoss, S. L. 1952. "A Study of Hebrew Vowels from Saadia Ga'on's Grammatical Work '*Kutub al-Lughah*,'" *JQR* 42, pp. 283–317.

— 1955. *Saadya Ga'on.* Philadelphia.

Sonne, I. 1944. "An Unknown Keroba of Yannai," *HUCA* 18, pp. 199–220.

Spanier, A. 1929. "Über Reste der palästinische Vokalization in Gebetsbüchern," *Monatsschrift für Geschichte und Wissenschaft Judentums* 73, pp. 472–5.

Sperber, A. 1938. "Hebrew Based upon Greek and Latin Transliterations," *HUCA* 12–13, pp. 103–274.

— 1959. *A Grammar of Masoretic Hebrew.* Copenhagen.

Talmon, S. 1964. "Aspects of the Textual Transmission of the Bible in the Light of Qumran Manuscripts," *Textus* IV, pp. 95–132.

Weil, G. 1962. "Un fragment de Okhlah palestinienne," *Annual of the Leeds University Oriental Society* III, pp. 68–80.

Weinreich, M. 1964. "The Origin of the Ashkenazic Pronunciation with Reference to Related Problems of Yiddish and Ashkenazic Hebrew," *Leshonenu* 27–8, pp. 131-47, 230–51, 318–39.

Yalon, H. 1964. *Introduction to the Pointing of the Mishna.* Jerusalem.

Yeivin, I. 1963. "A Palestinian Fragment of Haftaroth and Other MSS with Mixed Pointing," *Textus* 3, pp. 121–7.

Zulay, M. 1936. "Studies in Yannai," *Studies of the Research Institute for Hebrew Poetry* II, pp. 213–391.

Zunz, L. 1920. *Die synagogale Poesie des Mittelalters*, 2nd ed. Frankfurt a. M.

Ḥeth in Classical Hebrew

J. W. WEVERS

Everyone who has dabbled with Greek (hereafter G.) transliterations of Hebrew proper nouns knows that the Hebrew laryngeals *'aleph*, *he*, *ḥeth*, and *'ayin*, cannot be adequately represented by the Greek alphabet. Laryngeals are therefore represented in Greek transliterations by zero or by vowel mutations. It is also well known that the Canaanite (as well as the Aramaic) alphabet was ill-suited for representing all the phonemes of early South Canaanite. Thus the voiceless interdental spirant, /ð/, had no separate grapheme, and the *shīn* grapheme had to do double duty for itself as well as for the grooved palatal sibilant. Neither were there separate symbols for the voiced and voiceless velar spirants. These were represented by the graphemes for the voiced and voiceless pharyngeal spirants respectively, i.e. the *'ayin* and *ḥeth* symbols. Eventually the phonemic distinction between velar and pharyngeal spirants was lost, and velar spirants were no longer phonemic in Hebrew.

With respect to the voiced velar spirant /γ/, it is common knowledge that for certain place names it was transliterated by the Greek γ. Thus the etymological initial velar in *Gomorrah* and *Gaza* was transliterated by γ, but for the etymological initial pharyngeal in *Ekron* and *Ashkelon* zero was used. The relevance of these transliterations has usually been emphatically denied. Harris in his *Development of the Canaanite Dialects*[1] maintains that "the merging of these sets of phonemes may have taken place during the 11th or 10th century." He goes on to say, "Bergsträsser and others date the merging in the 4th century B.C., on the argument that the velar spirants were still 'remembered' in the Septuagint transcriptions.

1 Z. S. Harris, *Development of the Canaanite Dialects: An Investigation in Linguistic History* (*AOS* 16; New Haven: American Oriental Society, 1939), p. 63.

However, phonemes are not remembered once they cease to exist in a dialect; there is no satisfactory evidence that these phonemes existed in Palestine at the time of the LXX or for several centuries earlier. The LXX transcriptions with χ and γ cannot be used to prove [*ḫ*] and [γ] phonemes, for they are too frequently used in words which had etymological [ḥ] and [ʿ]."

This statement is at least in part based on the work of Ružička, who devoted more than one article to the thesis that the voiced velar spirant never existed in Proto-Semitic at all, and that its presence in Arabic constitutes a late dialectal development. In a lengthy article in *ZA* 21 (1908)[2] he examines the transliterations of *ʿayin/ghayin* in G. and concludes that the evidence was sporadic and that they show no evidence for the contemporary existence of a *ghayin* phone.

With approval he cites an earlier statement of Wallin,[3] who says: "Je mehr die Sprachen ausgebildet werden, desto mehr treten die Kehlbuchstaben in den Hinter- und die Lippenbuchstaben in den Vordergrund, wie dies, z.B., bei den romanischen Völkern u. den Engländern in hoherem Grade der Fall ist. Das Sprachinstrument schiebt sich, sozuzagen, immer mehr vorwärts, während es in roheren oder ursprünglichern Sprachen tiefer liegt." (Parenthetically it might be added that a velar is more *im Vordergrund* than a pharyngeal, though this is of course quite irrelevant. One notes also that the author wrote in German, presumably one of the *roheren oder ursprünglicheren Sprachen*!)

From all of this he concludes as follows: "Ich möchte nur hervorheben, dass, wie oben dargelegt wurde, der Übergang des *ghayin* in *ʿayin* physiologisch unerklärlich ist; er würde uns ja einen Übergang von einem leichteren zu einen schwereren Laute darstellen." This kind of statement is not competent, and every modern linguist would of course disregard any conclusions reached on the basis of it.

It should further be noted that all the transliterations are given by Ružička according to a single G. ms. (a notoriously bad one at that), and that he was not at all versed in the principles of text criticism. His lists are full of elementary errors, and each instance will have to be re-examined carefully. For example, he lists for the name *ʿtqṣyn* (Josh. 19:13) καтασεμ, which is the reading of ms. B

2 R. Ružička, "Ueber die Existenz des *Ghains* in Hebräischen," *ZA* 21 (1908), pp. 293–340.

3 G. A. Wallin, "Nachlese zur *G. A. Wallin's* über die Laute des Arabischen (Bd. IX, s. 1ff.)," *ZDMG* 12 (1858), p. 655.

(Cod. Vaticanus). Other readings to be taken into account are *κατσιμ*, *κασσιμ*, *και σημ*, *και σιν*, *κασειν*, *qšyn* (Syh), *Agisin* (Lat.), *CASI* (Sah.), *καιρ*, *κηρ*, and *κασιμ*. None of these readings represents the original transcription, however. The *κ* certainly does not represent the *ʿayin*, but rather the *qoph* (cf. *κασειν*, etc.). The original reading was probably *ατκασιμ* or *ατκασιν*, the transcription of *ατ* and *κ* producing *κατασιμ/ν*, from which the reading of B is easily obtained. It is accordingly clear that G. here transcribes the *ʿayin* by zero, which is etymologically what one might expect.

Another kind of error which is frequent in Ružička concerns the presumed transcription of final *ʿayin* by *kappa* in G. For example, the names *tʾrʿ/tḥrʿ* occur at 1 Chron. 8:35, 9:41. These are given as proof for confusion in G. since some mss. end the name with *κ/χ* whereas others omit it. (Actually only ms. p has *Θαρεκ* at 8:35 and all other mss. end with *ε/α*, whereas at 9:41 only mss. B S and c_2 read *Θαρεχ* and all others omit the final consonant.) The fact is that *κ/χ* is not original at all. In both passages the next word is *και*, and the letter came in by dittography; the correct transcription is *Θαρα/ε*.

Though Ružička's statement that the voiced velar spirant never existed in Proto-Semitic was itself never accepted by serious scholars, the conclusion that G.'s transliteration of *ʿayin* was thoroughly inconsistent was tacitly adopted; in fact it is now rather widely believed that the velar spirants had coalesced with the pharyngeal spirants long before the time of G. Eventually the work of Ružička on the transliterations of *ʿayin* in G. will have to be redone on a scientific basis. Meanwhile the subject of this inquiry is the transliteration of the grapheme *ḥeth* in G. as a means of testing the above hypothesis, *ḥeth* representing as it does the voiceless equivalent to the voiced *ʿayin*.

All the names in the OT containing the grapheme *ḥeth* (318) are listed below together with their Greek transcriptions. In each case all ms. variation has been considered and an attempt made to recover the original reading of G. In the rare case where the absence or presence of a *κ*, *χ*, or *κχ* as representing *ḥeth* was involved in such variation, it has been noted. The plus symbol after a G. transcription indicates other variants, usually in vowels. In no such case is *κ* or *χ* involved.

An attempt has been made to divide the names into /ħ/ and /χ/ groups. In those many instances where some doubt or complete uncertainty existed as to whether *ḥeth* represented /ħ/ or /χ/, the name was not used as evidence but rather placed in the "uncertain" or "unknown" class. The large number of proper names in these classes may be the result of excessive caution, but since many names may not even be Semitic in origin it was felt better to err in this direction.

A INSTANCES IN WHICH NAMES WITH ORIGINAL /ħ/ WERE TRANSLITERATED BY ZERO OR VOWEL MUTATION

(*'ḥy*)*šḥr* – (*Αχι*)*σααρ*. Cf. Ug. *šḥr*.
bḥwrym – *Βαουριμ*. √*bḥr*.
bḥr(*w*)*my* – *Βειρμι*.
(*byt*) *ḥglh* – *Εγλα*. Mod. *'ēn Ḥajla*.
(*byt*) *lḥm* – *Λεεμ*. √*lḥm*.
gḥm – *Γααμ*. Cf. Arab. *jaḥma*.
zbḥ – *Ζεβεε*. √*ðbḥ*.
zḥlt – *Ζωελεθ*. Cf. Arab. √*zḥl; zuḥal*.
ḥbb – *Ιωβαβ*. Cf. *ywbb* in 1 Chron. 8:9. √*ḥbb*.
ḥgy (1) – *Αγγαιος*. √*ḥgg*.
ḥgy (2) – *Αγγι*(*ς*).
ḥgyh – *Αγγια*.
ḥgyt – *Αγγιθ*.
ḥdš – *Αδα*(*ς*?). √*ḥdθ*.
ḥdšh – *Αδασα*.
ḥdšy – *Αδασαι*.
ḥwylh – *Ευιλα*(*θ*). √*ḥwl*.
ḥwl – *Ουλ*.
ḥwml – *Ιεμουηλ*. Wrong etymology; taken as *ḥmw'l*.
ḥwmly – *Ιερουηλι* +. Taken as *ḥmw'ly*.
ḥz'l – *Αζαηλ*. √*ḥzh*.
ḥzw – *Αζαυ*.
ḥzyh – *Οζια*.
ḥzyn – *Αζιν* +.
ḥzqy – *Αζακ*(*ε*)*ι*. √*ḥzq*.
ḥzqyhw – *Εζεκιας*.
ḥkmwny – *Αχαμανι*. √*ḥkm*.
ḥlḥwl – *Αλουα*. Mod. *Ḥalḥul*.
ḥmdn – *Αμαδα* +. Cf. Ug. and Arab. √*ḥmd*.
ḥmw'l – *Αμουηλ* – Luc.; lacking in G.
ḥmwr – *Εμμωρ*. Cf. Arab. *ḥimār*.
ḥmy/*wṭl* – *Αμειταλ*. Cf. Akk. *emu*, Arab. *ḥam*.
ḥmt (1) – *Αμ*(*μ*)*αθ*. √*ḥmm*.
ḥmt (2) – *Εμαθ* +.
ḥmt (3) – *Αιμαθ* +. Mod. *Ḥamā*.
ḥmt d'r – *Αμαθδωρ* +. Cf. *ḥmt* (1).
ḥmty – *Αμαθι*.
ḥndd – *Ηναδαδ*. As from *ḥn hdd*.
ḥnh – *Αννα*. √*ḥnn*.
ḥnwn – *Αναυν*.
ḥny'l – *Ανειηλ*.
ḥnn – *Αναν*.
ḥnn'l – *Ανανεηλ*.
ḥnny – *Ανανι*(*α*).
ḥnnyhw – *Ανανιας*.
ḥntn – *Εννωθων* +.
ḥpṣy bh – *Οφσιβα*. Cf. Arab. √*ḥpẓ*.
ḥpr (n. loc.) – *Οφερ* +. Cf. Arab. √*ḥpr*.
ḥpry – *Οφερι*.
ḥprym – *Αφεραιμ*.
ḥṣwr – *Ασωρ*. Cf. Ug. *ḥṣr*, Arab. *ḥaẓīra*.
ḥṣṣn tmr – *Ασασανθαμαρ*.
ḥṣr gdh – *Ασεργαδδα*.
ḥṣrwn – *Ασρων* +.
ḥṣrwt – *Ασηρωθ*.
ḥṣry – *Ασαραι*.
ḥṣrmwt – *Ασαρμωθ*.
ḥṣrny – *Ασρωνι*.
ḥṣr swsh – *Ασερσουσιμ*.
ḥṣr swsym – *Ασερσουσ*(*ε*)*ιμ*.
ḥṣr 'yn(*w*)*n* – *Ασερναιμ* +. Second element as from *n'ym*.

ḥṣr šw'l – *Ασερσωαλ* +.
ḥryp – *Αριφ*. Cf. Arab. √*ḥrf*.
ḥrš – *Αρης*. √*ḥrθ*. Cf. Ug. Arab. √*ḥrθ* and Akk. *erēšu*.
ḥrš' – *Αρησα*.
ḥršt – *Αρισωθ*.
ḥṣbnd – *Ασαβδανα*. √*ḥšb*.
ḥšbh – *Ασουβε* +.
ḥšbwn – *Εσεβων*.
ḥšbyh – *Ασαβια* +.
ḥšbnyh – *Ασαβανια*.
ḥšyb – *Ασουβ*.
yḥdy'l – *Ιεδιηλ*. √*yḥd*.
yḥdyhw – *Ιαδαια*.
yḥzyh – *Ιαζια*. √*ḥzh*.
yḥzq'l – *Ιεζεκιηλ*. √*ḥzq*.
yḥy'l – *Ιειηλ*. √*ḥyh*.
yḥy'ly – *Ιειηλ(ι)*.
yḥyh – *Ιεα(ια)*.
yḥmy – *Ια/εμαι*. √*ḥmh*.
yḥṣ'l – *Ασιηλ*. Cf. Arab. √*ḥẓy* and So. Arab. *ḥẓyh* cited by Noth, p. 204.[4]
yḥṣ'ly – *Ασιηλι*.
ypth – *Ιεφθα/ε*. √*pth*.
ypth-'l – *Ιφθαηλ*.
yšbh – *Ιεσβα*. √*šbḥ*.
lwḥyt – *Λουειθ* +. Cf. Arab. √*lwḥ*.
lḥmy – *Λεεμι*.
lqḥy – *Λο/υκεειμ*. Cf. Ug., Arab., Eth. √*lqḥ*, and Akk. *leqû*.
mḥwy'l – *Μαιηλ*. As though *mḥy'l*.
mḥzy'wt – *Μεαζωθ*. √*ḥzh*.
mḥlh – *Μααλα* +. Cf. Arab. √*mḥl*.
mḥlwn – *Μααλων*. G. understood √*mḥl* wrongly.
mḥly – *Μοολι*. Cf. *mḥlh*.
mḥlt – *Μολλαθ/Μαελεθ*.
nḥly'l – *Νααλιηλ*. √*nḥl*.
nḥmyh – *Νεεμια(ς)*. √*nḥm*.
nḥmny – *Ναεμανι*.
nḥš – *Ναας*. Cf. Arab. √*nḥs*; probably understood as 'copper red.'
nḥšwn – *Νaασσων*.
nḥšt – *Νεσθα*.
nḥštn – *Νεεσθαν*.
nptwḥ – *Ναφθω*. √*ptḥ*.
plḥ – *Φελλαιε*. √*plḥ*.
pqḥ – *Φακεε*. √*pqḥ*.
pqḥyh – *Φακειας*.
ptḥyh – *Φε/αθαια*. √*ptḥ*.
ṣḥr – *Σααρ*. Cf. Arab. *ṣaḥra*.
qrḥ (1) – *Καρηε*. √*qrḥ*; cf. Arab., Eth.
qrḥ (2) – *Κορε(ε)* +.
qrḥy – *Κορειται* or (*υιος*) *Κορε*.
rḥb (1) – *Ρααβ* (but *Ραχαβ* in Matt. 1:5.). √*rḥb*.
rḥb (2) – *Ρααβ/Ροωβ*.
rḥbwt – *Ροωβωθ*.
rḥbyh – *Ρααβια*.
rḥb'm – *Ροβοαμ*.
rḥwm – *Ραουμ*. √*rḥm*.
rḥm – *Ραεμ*.
šḥryh – *Σααρια*. Cf. Ug. *šḥr*.
šḥrym – *Σααρημ*.
tḥnh – *Θανα*+. √*ḥnn*.
tḥt – *Θααθ*. √*tḥt*.

B INSTANCES WHERE ORIGINAL /χ/ WERE TRANSLITERATED IN G. BY χ OR κ

'ḥwḥ – *Αχια*. G. read *'ḥyh* from √*'āχ*.
'ḥwmy – *Αχειμαι*. Cf. Akk. *Aχumma* (Ebeling, *Reallex. d. Assyr.* I p. 58).
'ḥz – *Αχαζ*. √*'χð*.
'ḥzm – *Ωχαζαμ*
'ḥzy – *Αχαζιου*.
'ḥzyh(w) – *Οχοζειας*.
'ḥzt – *Οχοζας*.

4 M. Noth, *Die israelitischen Personennamen im Rahmen der gemeinsemitischen Nahmengebung*, *BWANT*, 3e Folge, Heft 10 (Stuttgart: W. Kohlhammer, 1928).

'ḥy'm – Αχιαμ. A compound with /'āχ/.
'ḥyh – Αχια.
'ḥyhwd – Αχιωρ.
'ḥy(ḥd) – Αχιχυδ.
(*'ḥy*)*ḥd* – Cf. Akk. *χi'ādu*, a kind of speaking prob. related to Heb. *ḥīdā*; cf. *Arch. f. Or.* 19, p. 58: 129.
'ḥyṭwb – Αχιτωβ. Cf. *'ḥy'm*.
'ḥylwd – Αχιλουδ +.
'ḥymwt – Αχιμωθ.
'ḥymlk – Αχιμελεχ.
'ḥymn – Αχιμαν (tris, sed Αιμαν ad 1 Chron. 9:17 = *ḥymn?*).
'ḥym'ṣ – Αχιμαας.
'ḥyndb – Αχιναδαβ.
'ḥyn'm – Αχιναμ.
'ḥysmk – Αχισαμαχ.
'ḥy'zr – Αχιεζερ.
'ḥyqm – Αχικαμ.
'ḥyrm – Αχιραν.
'ḥyrmy – Αχιρανι +.
'ḥyr' – Αχειρε.
'ḥy(šḥr) – Αχισααρ.
'ḥyšr – Αχιηλ. (G. Luc., sed Hex. – Αχισαρ.)
'ḥytpl – Αχιτοφελ.
'ḥly – Αχλαι. At least G. understood as from / *'āḥ* /.
ḥbr (1) – Χαβερ +. √*χbr*.
ḥbr (2) – Χαβερ.
ḥbry – Χοβερι.
ḥbrwn – Χεβρων.
ḥdd – Χοδδαδ. Cf. *χudadu* (Aram. tribe).
ḥdly – Χοδλι. √*χdl*.
ḥwtm – Χωθαμ. √*χtm*.
ḥlbwn – Χελβων. Mod. *Xalbūn;* √*χlb*.
ḥldy – Χελδαι. √*χld*.
ḥlṣ – Χελλης. √*χlṣ;* cf. So. Arab. *χlṣt*.
ḥlq – Χελεκ +. √*χlq*.
ḥlqy (1) – Χελεκι.
ḥlqy (2) – Χελκιας.
ḥlqyhw – Χελκιας.
ḥlqt – Χελκαθ +.
ḥm – Χαμ. Cf. *χammu* (*HUC* 18, pp. 473 ff.).
ḥy'l – Αχιηλ. G. read *'ḥy'l* as from / *'āχ* /.
ḥrb – Χωρηλ. Cf. Ug. *χrb*, Akk. *χarabū*, and Arab. √*χrb*.
ḥry – Χορραιος. Cf. *χurru*.
ḥrn – Χαρραν. Cf. Akk. *χarrānu*.
(*h*)*ḥrsyt* – Χαρσειθ. √*χrs*.
ḥty – Χετταιος. Cf. *χatti*.
ṭbḥ – Ταβεκ/χ. √*ṭbχ*.
ṭbḥt – Ταβηχα(ς).
yrḥ – Ιεραχ (but Luc. has Ιαρε at 1 Chron. 1:20). √*yrχ*.
klḥ – Κ/Χαλαχ. Cf. Akk. *Kalχu*.
mḥyr – Μαχιρ. Cf. Akk. *Maχur-ili; Maχir-aχa-iddin; Maχir-iqbi*.
nḥwr – Ναχωρ. √*nχr*. Cf. Ug. *'anχr;* also Ass. names *Naχara'u, Niχaru* (name of desert king; cf. Borger, *Arch. f. Or.* Beih. 9, p. 56).
swḥ – Σουχι. Cf. Akk. *Suχu*.
snḥryb – Σανναχειρειμ. G. understood / *'āχ* / correctly.
rḥl – Ραχηλ. √*rχl*.

C INSTANCES WHERE ZERO OR VOWEL MUTATION IN G. PROBABLY REPRESENTS AN ORIGINAL ḫ

bryḥ – Βερια. Noth (p. 227) cites Arab. *barīχ*, a lexical word, prob. an error for *barīḥ*. The root *brḥ* is well known.

ḥdyd – *Αδιδ*. Prob. / ħ /; cf. Akk. *edēdu*, Arab. *ḥadd*.

ḥwr – *Ουρ/Ωρ*. Cf. Arab. *ḥāra*. Though √*χwr* also exists, the root with / ħ / is here likely.

ḥwry – *Ουρι*.

ḥwrm – *Ωριμ*. G. took this name as pl. of *ḥwry*.

ḥwrn – *Αυρανιτις*. Cf. Arab. *ḥawrān*, Ug. *ḥrn*, but Ak. *χaurān*. Caution on accepting an Akk. transcription of words non-Akk. in origin must be exercised. The original phoneme was prob. / ħ /.

ḥkylh – *Εχελα*. Hebrew phonotactics would make the consecution of / χκ / most unlikely. Cf. also Arab. √*ḥkl*.

ḥklyh – *Αχελια*.

ḥmwn – *Αμων*. In 1 Chron. 6:61 G. has *χαμων* but Hex. corrects to *Αμμων*. √*ḥmm*.

ḥnwk – *Ενωχ* +. The root *ḥnk* is well known and is here relevant. The occurrence of Can. *χanaku* must be viewed in the light of the comment on *ḥwrn*.

ḥrym – *Ηραμ* +. Cf. Arab., Eth. √*ḥrm* and Ug. pr. n. (*bn*) *ḥrm*. The Akk. √*χrm* shows how sceptically the writing of even native words in cuneiform must be treated.

ḥrm – *Αρειμ* +.

ḥrmh – *Ερμα* +.

ḥrmwn – *Αερμων*.

yḥzrh – *Ιεζριου* +. Comp. Arab. √*ḥḏr*.

nṣyḥ – *Νεισεια*. Comp. Arab. *naṣīḥ*.

D INSTANCES WHERE κ OR χ IN G. PROBABLY REPRESENTS AN ORIGINAL χ

ʾḥy – *Αγκις/ν* Ms. HP 84 has *αχι* which could be G.

E NAMES WITH *ḥeth* OF UNCERTAIN ETYMOLOGIES

ʾrḥ (1) – *Ορεχ*. The root with / χ / is well known and appears as *ʾrḥ* (1), but roots with / ħ / are equally possible.

ʾrḥ (2) – *Ηρα/Αρες*.

gyḥ – *Γαι*. Cf. Arab. *jāʾiḥu* though the root *jwχ* might seem more relevant.

zrḥ – *Ζα/ηρα*. This is probably / ħ / as √*ðrḥ* in So. Arab. n. pr. shows.

zrḥy – *Ζαραει*.

zrḥyh – *Ζαραια*.

ḥṭyl – *Αττιλ* +. Both roots *χṭl* and *ḥṣl* could be considered.

ḥlb – *Αλαφ* +. The roots *ħlb* and *χlb* are both well known.

ḥlbh – *Χελβα/Ελβα* (Judg. 1:31).

ḥlp – *Αλεφ*. Roots with / ħ / and / χ / both existed.

ḥph – 1 Chron. 24:13. B trad. *Χοφφα;* A trad. *Οφφα*. Uncertain etymology since both roots are known.

ḥpym – *Αφφειμ*.

ḥpr (n. pr.) – *Οφερ*. As a personal name (cf. note on *ḥpr* – n. loc. under A above) the root *χpr* is also possible.

ḥrwṣ – *Αρους* (II Kings 21:19). Ass. name *χarruṣu*. But Arab. √*ḥrḍ* could also be considered, though *χrṣ* seems more likely.

ḥšm (1) – *Ησαμ* +. Usually Arab. *χaθīm* is cited as cognate, but *ḥaθma* is equally appropriate.

ḥšm (2) – *Ασομ* +.

ḥtt – *Αθαθ*. Both roots *ħtt* and *χtt* are known.

lḥy – *Λεχει* (Judg. 15:9). Cod. B: *Λευει* is result of corruption in uncial transmission. Note Arab. *laḥy*, Ug. *lḥm*, but Akk. *laχû*.

nbḥ – *Ναβου/αι*. Arab., Eth. √*nbḥ* but Akk. √*nbχ*.

nbḥz – *Ναιβας* +. If as sometimes conjectured the name is from *zbḥ*, the original phoneme was / ħ /. But it is doubtful that G. knew this.

nbḥy – *Ναβι*. Both roots *nħb* and nχ*b* existed.

nḥt (1) – *Ναχε/οθ*. In I Chron. 1:37, Gen. 36:13, 17 one person.

nḥt (2) *Νααλεθ*. Two other people: I Chron. 6:11 and II Chron. 31:13. Both roots with / ħ / and / χ / were known. Cf. discussion under section I.

pḥt (*mw'b*) – *Φααθμωαβ* +. Roots with / ħ / and / χ / are attested.

šwḥ – *Σωε* +. Roots with / ħ / and / χ / are known.

šwḥh – *Ασμα* (I Chron. 4:11).

šwḥym – *Σαυχειης* +.

šlḥ (1) – *Σαλα*. Arab. *salāḥ* and Ug. *šlḥ* are likely cognate, but for *šlḥ* (2) Akk. *šalāχu* might be relevant.

šlḥ (2) – *Σειλωαμ*. Though the note on *šlḥ* (1) may be correct, it is irrelevant since the single occurrence (Neh. 3:15) is not transliterated but interpreted as *Siloam.*

šlḥy – *Σαλει* +.

šlḥym – *Σελεειμ*.

šrḥ – *Σα(α)ρ(ρ)α*. Cf. Sab. *šrḥ* but Ass. *Surχu*.

F NAMES WITH *ḥeth* WHERE THE ETYMOLOGY IS UNKNOWN

'zrḥy – *Ισραηλιτης*. Misunderstood by G. as *yzr"ly?*

'hwḍ – *Αωδ*. Prob. read as *'hwd.*

'ḥwḥy – *Αχωχι*.

'ḥyn – *Αιμ* +. Understood as an Aram. word?

'ḥlb – *Αλαφ*.

'ḥsby – *Ασβιτου*.

'ḥrḥ – *Αρα*.

gḥzy – *Γιεζι*.

zwḥt – *Ζωχαθ*.

znwḥ – *Ζανω*.

ḥbqwq – *Αμβακουμ*.

ḥgb – *Αγαβ*.

ḥgb' – *Αγαβα*. (Aram.)

ḥdrk – *Αδρακ*. (Zech. 9:1). Since this is the Hebrew transcription (through Aram.?) of Akk. (*χatarikka*), G. is hardly evidence.

ḥwbh – *Χωβα*.

ḥwy – *Ευαιος*.

ḥwpm – *Οφιμιν*.

ḥwpmy – *Σωφανι* (?)

ḥwšh – *Ουσαθι* +.

ḥwšy – *Χουσι*.

ḥwšym – *Ωσιμ*.

ḥlḥ – *Αλαε* (II Kings 17:6; 8:11), *Χαλαχ* (I Chron. 5:26).

ḥly – *Αλει* (?)

ḥṭyṭ' – *Ατητα* +. (Aram.)

ḥṭyp' – *Ατουφα*. (Aram.)

ḥṭwš – *Αττους* (4 times, but I Chron.

3:22 – *Χαττους*, with *Ατ(τ)ους(ε)* as variant texts).
ḥl'h – *Αλαα* +.
ḥmṭh – *Ευμα*.
ḥnm'l – *Αναμεηλ*.
ḥsdyh – *Ασαδια*.
ḥsh – *Οσσα* +.
ḥsrh – *Εσερη*. Cod. B uniquely has *Χελλης*, which represents a different name tradition.
ḥpny – *Οφνι*. (Eg.)
ḥpr' – *Ουαφρη*. (Eg.)
ḥqwp' – *Ακουφα*. (Aram.)
ḥrbwn' – *Αρβωνα(ς)*. (Aram.)
ḥrd – *Αρωεδ* +.
ḥrdh – *Χαραδαθ*.
ḥrwdy – *Αρωδαιος*.
ḥrwmp – *Ερωμαφ* +.
ḥrwnym – *Αρωνιιμ* +.
ḥrḥyh – *Αραχιου*.
ḥrnpr – *Αρνεφαρ*. (Eg.)
ḥrs – *Αρες*.
ḥrp – *Αρειμ*. (?)
ḥrt – *Αριθ* +.
ḥšwp' – *Ασουφα* +. (Aram.)
ḥšmwn – *Ασεμων* +.
ḥšmwnh – *Ασεμωνα* +.
yḥl'l(y) – *Αλοηλ/Αλληλ(ι)*.
yḥmy – *Ιεμου*.
yḥt – *Ιε(ε)θ*.
yryḥw – *Ιερειχω*.
lḥms – Josh. 15:40: B text, *Μαχες* (as though *mḥs*); A text, *Λαμας*.
mḥwym – *Μαωνι*.
mḥwl – *Μαουλ*.
mḥyd' – *Μειδα* +. (Aram.)
mḥlty – *Μοουλαθι*.
mḥt – *Μεθ/Μααθ*.
syḥwn – *Σηων*. Amor. name into Hebrew.
prwḥ – *Φουασουδ*. G. read a different text.
pšḥwr – *Πασχωρ* +. (Eg.)
ṣyḥ' – *Σηα* +. (Prob. Aram.)
ṣlpḥd – *Σαλπααδ*.
šwḥmy – *Σαμε(ι)* +.
šḥṣym – *Σασιμα*.
šyḥwr – *Σειωρ*. (Eg.)
tḥpnḥs – *Ταφναι*. (Eg.)
tḥpnys – *Θεχεμεινα*. (Eg.)
tḥr – *Θαραα*.
tlḥ – *Θαλα*.
tmḥ – *Θεμα*.
tpwḥ – *Θαπους* +.

G ORIGINAL /ħ/ RENDERED BY *κ* OR *χ* IN G.

nḥm – *Ναχεμ*. Possibly G. understood this as the biliteral √*χm*.
tḥn – *Ταναχ* (at Num. 26:35); *Θαεμ* correctly at 1 Chron. 7:25. The transcription of this word and the next in the Num. passage is based on a metathesis of [ḥ] and [ṇ]; it is an error and not evidence of confusion of / ħ / and / χ /.
tḥny – *Ταναχι* (Num. 26:35 only).

H ORIGINAL /χ/ RENDERED BY ZERO OR VOWEL MUTATION IN G.

gyḥwn – *Γηων* +. Possibly a root with / χ / (cf. Arab. √*jwχ;* reference to Akk. *guχχu* is probably irrelevant) is original. It could, however, be a pre-Semitic place name.
ḥbwr – *Αβωρ* (tris), but *Χαβωρ* – 1 Chron. 5:26 rightly.

ḥbr – *Αβε/αρ* (bis).
ḥld – *Αλαδ* (1 Chron. 11:30 only). Cf. Arab. √*χld*.
ḥldh – *Ολδα* (bis).
yrwḥ – *Ιδαι* (1 Chron. 5:14). Misread [r] as [d].
mḥnym – *Μαναεμ* +. This would seem clearly to be / χ /; cf. Akk. *χanû*, but cf. its Mod. equivalent (and possible location ?) at *Khirbet Maḥneh* near Ajlūn.
nḥry – *Νααραι* (1 Chron. 11:39) but Cod. B : *Ναχωρ*. Cf. also Arab. √*nḥr*.
trḥ – *Θαρ(ρ)α*.

I INCONSISTENCIES

In the case of the biliteral root *nḥ* both roots *nħ* and *nχ* occur in weak Semitic verbs (cf. Hebrew *nwḥ* and *nḥh*). Hence some confusion was possible in the following names. These names accordingly are not put forward as evidence.

nwḥ – *Νωε* +.
nwḥh – *Νωα* +.
ynwḥ – *Ιανωχ*.
ynwḥh – *Ιανωχα* +.
mnwḥ – *Μανωε*.
mnḥt – *Μαχαναθει/Μαναχαθ*.
mnḥty – *Μαναθ* +.

J CONCLUSIONS

In tabular form the following results have been obtained.

	Hebrew				Greek	
Section	Orig./ħ/	Orig./χ/	Uncertain	Unknown	Zero	By κ/χ
A	121				121	
B		61				61
C	17				17	
D		1				1
E			32		27 (25)	7 (5)
F				73	62	11
G	3					3
H		9			9	

Sections E and F contain 105 names of uncertain or unknown etymology and might well be disregarded. If sections A, C, and G as well as B, D, and H are totalled, there are 141 names with original /ħ/ and 71 with /χ/.

NAMES	TRANSLITERATION	
	Zero	κ/χ
141 with /ħ/	138	3
71 with /χ/	9	62

Phonotactically *ḥeth* (both as original velar and as pharyngeal) obtains between juncture and V, intervocalic, between C and V, between V and C, and between V and juncture. It is comparatively infrequent in the last category, i.e. in word final position. With respect to the possible phonemic distinction between /ħ/ and /χ/ the phonotactics of the language appear to be without significance. This appears from the random examples listed below:

As V–	*ḥgy*	– *Αγγαιος*
	ḥnwn	– *Ανουν*
As –VV–	*yḥy'l*	– *Ιειηλ*
	yḥzq'l	– *Ιεζεκιηλ*
As –V	*yšbḥ*	– *Ιεσβα*
	pqḥ	– *Φακεε*
As C–	*ḥbrwn*	– *Χεβρων*
	ḥlqyhw	– *Χελκιας*
As –C–	*rḥl*	– *Ραχηλ*
	'ḥyqm	– *Αχικαμ*
As –C	*tbḥ*	– *Ταβεκ/χ*
	yrḥ	– *Ιεραχ*

Of the three /ħ/ names incorrectly rendered by χ in G. two occur at Num. 26:35, where the names *tḥn* and *tḥny* were misread by metathesis as *tnḥ* and *tnḥy* (cf. section 1) and are not evidential. The name *tḥn* also occurs at 1 Chron. 7:25, where it appears correctly as *Θαεμ*. The third name, *nḥm*, is a *hapax legomenon* (1 Chron. 4:19) and may have been wrongly understood as derived from √*χm*.

Of the nine /χ/ names incorrectly rendered by zero or vowel mutation in G. the name *trḥ* is especially puzzling (13 occurrences) since its etymology with /χ/ seems clear. The other frequently occurring name (14 times) is the n. loc. *Mahanaim*, but its etymology is rendered suspect by the mod. name of *Khirbet Maḥneh. Gihon* occurs five times; it is apparently a very old name (cf. its occurrence as one of the rivers of Eden, Gen. 2:13); if it is pre-Semitic, it is hardly evidence. Of the other six names, one occurs three times; two, twice; and three only once. At least one of these is a misreading by G.

On the other hand, 138 names with etymological /ħ/ are transliterated correctly by zero or vowel mutation, and 62 names with etymological /χ/, by Greek κ or χ. Furthermore, these include such well-known names as *Bethlehem*, *Haggai*, *Hezekiah*, *Hamath*, *Hazor*, *Nehemiah*, *Rahab*, and *Rehoboam* (all containing /ħ/) and *Ahaz*, *Ahijah*,*Hebron*, *Hilkiah*, *Hurrian*, and *Hittite* (all with original /χ/) – names which occur frequently throughout the OT but are always transliterated in G. consistent with their etymological origin.

It is therefore clear from the hundreds, in fact thousands, of instances of consistent transcriptions of /ħ/ by zero or vowel mutation and of /χ/ by Greek κ or χ that the voiceless velar and pharyngeal spirants were not "remembered phonemes" as Bergsträsser maintained, but were still phonemically distinct at the time and place of the Old Greek translation, i.e. as late as the second century B.C. No other conclusion fits the evidence.

This conclusion may well have further implications for the phonemic inventory of the Hebrew of the second century B.C. The possible, if not probable, phonemic distinctiveness of /γ/ versus /ʿ/, i.e. of the voiced equivalents to /χ/ and /ħ/, will have to be retested. A preliminary re-examination of the work done by Ružička has led the author to a tentative thesis that the /γ/ phoneme was in process of being lost at precisely this time.

A second possible implication concerns the spirantization of the non-emphatic stops /b, g, d, k, p, t/. It would seem likely, as Harris suggests,[5] that this took place (at least for /k, g/) after /γ/ and /χ/ had been assimilated by /ʿ/ and /ħ/ respectively. Since the evidence for this change is mainly late Phoenician, the suggestion that the spirantization of non-emphatic stops did not become phonemic before the second century B.C. is not at all out of order.[6]

5 Harris, *Development of the Canaanite Dialects*, p. 66.

6 I am particularly grateful to my colleagues Professors A. K. Grayson and G. M. Wickens for their many suggestions, especially in their respective fields of Akkadian and Arabic.

Printed in Belgium

PRINTED IN BELGIUM
BY
THE ST. CATHERINE PRESS, LTD.
TEMPELHOF, 37, BRUGES